Middle School Writing for the Common Core

Related Titles

Middle School Algebra for the Common Core
Middle School Geometry for the Common Core
Middle School Reading for the Common Core

Middle School Writing for the Common Core

LEARNINGEXPRESS ®

NEW YORK

Copyright © 2016 LearningExpress.

All rights reserved under International and Pan-American Copyright Conventions. Published in the United States by LearningExpress, New York.

Cataloging-in-Publication Data is on file with the Library of Congress.

ISBN 978-1-61103-047-1

Printed in the United States of America

9 8 7 6 5 4 3 2 1

For more information on LearningExpress, other LearningExpress products, or bulk sales, please write us at:
    224 W. 29th Street
    3rd Floor
    New York, NY 10001

Contents

Contents

Contents

Introduction

Welcome—and congratulations on your decision to improve your writing skills! Your commitment is itself an important part of learning to write well. Articulating your thoughts and feelings using the written word can be a mysterious process, so a willingness to stick through your confusion and any setbacks is necessary to success. And the rewards are great. Solid writing skills are crucial to success in just about every academic discipline and many, many professions. Furthermore, what can be more satisfying than engaging an audience with your insights—or better yet, getting your readers to laugh, or to cry?

In this book, we'll be focusing on the writing skills described and required by the Common Core State Standards (CCSS).

What Are the Common Core State Standards?

The introduction of the CCSS has resulted in many changes in American public schools—and not a little controversy. Some of the controversy is based on misinformation, so before we get started, let's take a look at the standards. What are they, really? Why were they developed, and how are they being implemented?

What?

The CCSS is a set of goals. These goals, or standards, tell what students at each grade level should be able to do at the end of the year. The CCSS sets standards for students in two subject areas: English Language Arts and Mathematics. Additionally, there are standards for reading and writing in history, social studies, science, and technical subjects.

When you think of the CCSS, keep the meaning of the word *goal* in mind. A goal is a result or achievement, not a path. The CCSS doesn't say much about how to meet the standards it sets. There are no required methods, textbooks, or curriculum. The CCSS is based on an underlying philosophy, however, that values more in-depth learning and flexible and critical thinking.

Who?

Three organizations led the effort to develop the CCSS: Achieve, the National Governors Association Center for Best Practices (NGA Center), and the Council of Chief State School Officers (CCSSO). Achieve is a nonprofit that was founded by a group of governors and business leaders in 1996. Its mission includes raising academic standards in the United States. The NGA Center is a consulting firm that advises governors on public policy. The CCSSO is the professional organization for statewide education leaders, such as state superintendents. Through their membership in these organizations, governors and state education leaders in 48 states, two territories, and the District of Columbia participated in the development of the CCSS, as did teachers, both formally and informally, in a number of ways.

The standards were neither developed nor mandated by the federal government, and the decision whether or not to adopt the standards is made by each state.

Why?

On the whole, the performance of students in the United States on international assessments of math, reading, and science is about average: neither terrible nor great. A closer look at the data, however, reveals that the students in some states are able to do very well on these tests, whereas the students in other states are not. One aim of creating a challenging "common core" of standards is to build an internationally competitive and more nationally unified educational system.

Another aim of the standards is to produce high school graduates who are—as the slogan goes—"college and career ready." In other words, the goal is for students to complete their high school education prepared to meet the challenges of college or the workplace.

When?

An educational reform movement focused on the creation of academic standards began in the 1980s, and throughout the 1990s, with support from the federal government, both states and professional organizations for educators created and adopted academic standards. The CCSS could be seen as the culmination of this movement. The drafting process began in 2009, a draft was officially released for public comment in March 2010, and the final version was published in June 2010.

Where?

More than 40 states have adopted the CCSS, in addition to the District of Columbia, four territories, and the Department of Defense Education Activity.

How?

The CCSS outline goals for students; curricula and lesson plans organize and outline the classroom activities that enable students to meet these goals. In states where the CCSS have been adopted, district and school administrators and teachers develop curricula and lesson plans aimed at the learning outcomes described in the CCSS.

The activities in this book, too, are aimed at the learning outcomes described in the CCSS for English Language Arts.

The English Language Arts Standards

The English Language Arts CCSS organize the study of English Language Arts in four broad categories:

- Reading

- Writing

- Speaking and Listening

- Language

This book is concerned with the writing standards and relevant language standards for middle school (grades 6–8).

The Standards for Writing

The writing standards emphasize three text types: arguments, informative/explanatory texts, and narratives. (Poetry and other forms of creative writing are not included.) The standards describe the elements of strong writing: development, organization, style, and a sense of purpose and audience. They also affirm the value of the writing process, research, and the use of relevant, well-chosen evidence.

The Standards for Language

About half of the language standards have to do with the conventions of standard English, including concerns with grammar, usage, capitalization, punctuation, and spelling. These concerns are not only with the *correct* use of language but with the *effective* use of language, as well as an understanding that what is perceived to be acceptable language use varies according to context.

The other half of the language standards have to do with vocabulary and are not treated in this book.

How to Use This Book

The idea behind this book is similar to the one taught by Aesop's tortoise: steady effort, even just a bit at a time, leads to success. Each of the 30 lessons in this book takes only about 15 minutes to complete. By working on the lessons regularly—one per day, for example, or two or three per week—you'll come to a better understanding of the writing process and the elements of clear, engaging writing.

Each lesson includes an overview of the topic or skill, relevant examples, and one or more practice exercises. The lessons themselves are grouped in sections that lead you through the writing process—from setting your purpose for writing to publishing your final composition.

Each time you sit down to work on one of the lessons, remember the following:

- Your best work will get done without distractions! Turn off your phone and TV, and resist the urge to browse the Internet.

- Have paper and a pen or pencil handy so that you can do the practice exercises.

- Also have a timer handy for timed writing exercises. You might also want to set your timer for 15 minutes at the start of each lesson. Set yourself the challenge of working without interruption during that time!

Correlations to the English Language Arts Standards

The charts on this and the following pages show how the lessons in the book correlate with the Common Core State Standards for Writing and Language (standards 1–3).

Common Core State Standards for Writing			Lesson
W.6.1, W.7.1, W.8.1 Write arguments to support claims with clear reasons and relevant evidence.			**Lesson 1:** What's Your Purpose?
W.6.1a Introduce claim(s) and organize the reasons and evidence clearly.	**W.7.1a** Introduce claim(s), acknowledge alternate or opposing claims, and organize the reasons and evidence logically.	**W.8.1a** Introduce claim(s), acknowledge and distinguish the claim(s) from alternate or opposing claims, and organize the reasons and evidence logically.	**Lesson 7:** Defining and Developing Your Thesis **Lesson 8:** Outlining **Lesson 9:** Organizational Patterns **Lesson 11:** Beginning Your Draft **Lesson 12:** Writing the Introduction
W.6.1b Support claim(s) with clear reasons and relevant evidence, using credible sources and demonstrating an understanding of the topic or text.	**W.7.1b** Support claim(s) with logical reasoning and relevant evidence, using accurate, credible sources and demonstrating an understanding of the topic or text.	**W.8.1b** Support claim(s) with logical reasoning and relevant evidence, using accurate, credible sources and demonstrating an understanding of the topic or text.	**Lesson 5:** Defining and Developing Your Topic **Lesson 13:** Writing the Body Paragraphs
W.6.1c Use words, phrases, and clauses to clarify the relationships among claim(s) and reasons.	**W.7.1c** Use words, phrases, and clauses to create cohesion and clarify the relationships among claim(s), reasons, and evidence.	**W.8.1c** Use words, phrases, and clauses to create cohesion and clarify the relationships among claim(s), counterclaims, reasons, and evidence.	**Lesson 18:** Editing Your Writing: Habits to Adopt
W.6.1d Establish and maintain a formal style.	**W.7.1d** Establish and maintain a formal style.	**W.8.1d** Establish and maintain a formal style.	**Lesson 12:** Writing the Introduction **Lesson 17:** Editing Your Writing: Habits to Avoid
W.6.1e Provide a concluding statement or section that follows from the argument presented.	**W.7.1e** Provide a concluding statement or section that follows from and supports the argument presented.	**W.8.1e** Provide a concluding statement or section that follows from and supports the argument presented.	**Lesson 15:** Writing a Strong Conclusion
W.6.2, W.7.2, W.8.2 Write informative/explanatory texts to examine a topic and convey ideas, concepts, and information through the selection, organization, and analysis of relevant content.			**Lesson 1:** What's Your Purpose?

Common Core State Standards for Writing			Lesson
W.6.2a Introduce a topic; organize ideas, concepts, and information, using strategies such as definition, classification, comparison/contrast, and cause/effect; include formatting (e.g., headings), graphics (e.g., charts, tables), and multimedia when useful to aiding comprehension.	**W.7.2a** Introduce a topic clearly, previewing what is to follow; organize ideas, concepts, and information, using strategies such as definition, classification, comparison/contrast, and cause/effect; include formatting (e.g., headings), graphics (e.g., charts, tables), and multimedia when useful to aiding comprehension.	**W.8.2a** Introduce a topic clearly, previewing what is to follow; organize ideas, concepts, and information into broader categories; include formatting (e.g., headings), graphics (e.g., charts, tables), and multimedia when useful to aiding comprehension.	**Lesson 7:** Defining and Developing Your Thesis **Lesson 8:** Outlining **Lesson 9:** Organizational Patterns **Lesson 11:** Beginning Your Draft **Lesson 12:** Writing the Introduction **Lesson 18:** Editing Your Writing: Habits to Adopt
W.6.2b Develop the topic with relevant facts, definitions, concrete details, quotations, or other information and examples.	**W.7.2b** Develop the topic with relevant facts, definitions, concrete details, quotations, or other information and examples.	**W.8.2b** Develop the topic with relevant, well-chosen facts, definitions, concrete details, quotations, or other information and examples.	**Lesson 5:** Defining and Developing Your Topic **Lesson 13:** Writing the Body Paragraphs
W.6.2c Use appropriate transitions to clarify the relationships among ideas and concepts.	**W.7.2c** Use appropriate transitions to create cohesion and clarify the relationships among ideas and concepts.	**W.8.2c** Use appropriate and varied transitions to create cohesion and clarify the relationships among ideas and concepts.	**Lesson 18:** Editing Your Writing: Habits to Adopt
W.6.2d Use precise language and domain-specific vocabulary to inform about or explain the topic.	**W.7.2d** Use precise language and domain-specific vocabulary to inform about or explain the topic.	**W.8.2d** Use precise language and domain-specific vocabulary to inform about or explain the topic.	**Lesson 18:** Editing Your Writing: Habits to Adopt
W.6.2e Establish and maintain a formal style.	**W.7.2e** Establish and maintain a formal style.	**W.8.2e** Establish and maintain a formal style.	**Lesson 12:** Writing the Introduction **Lesson 17:** Editing Your Writing: Habits to Avoid
W.6.2f Provide a concluding statement or section that follows from the information or explanation presented.	**W.7.2f** Provide a concluding statement or section that follows from and supports the information or explanation presented.	**W.8.2f** Provide a concluding statement or section that follows from and supports the information or explanation presented.	**Lesson 15:** Writing a Strong Conclusion
W.6.3, W.7.3, W.8.3 Write narratives to develop real or imagined experiences or events using effective technique, relevant descriptive details, and well-structured event sequences.			**Lesson 1:** What's Your Purpose?

Common Core State Standards for Writing			Lesson
W.6.3a Engage and orient the reader by establishing a context and introducing a narrator and/or characters; organize an event sequence that unfolds naturally and logically.	**W.7.3a** Engage and orient the reader by establishing a context and point of view and introducing a narrator and/or characters; organize an event sequence that unfolds naturally and logically.	**W.8.3a** Engage and orient the reader by establishing a context and point of view and introducing a narrator and/or characters; organize an event sequence that unfolds naturally and logically.	**Lesson 7:** Defining and Developing Your Thesis **Lesson 8:** Outlining **Lesson 9:** Organizational Patterns **Lesson 11:** Beginning Your Draft **Lesson 12:** Writing the Introduction
W.6.3b Use narrative techniques, such as dialogue, pacing, and description, to develop experiences, events, and/or characters.	**W.7.3b** Use narrative techniques, such as dialogue, pacing, and description, to develop experiences, events, and/or characters.	**W.8.3b** Use narrative techniques, such as dialogue, pacing, description, and reflection, to develop experiences, events, and/or characters.	**Lesson 5:** Defining and Developing Your Topic **Lesson 14:** Writing the Body of a Narrative
W.6.3c Use a variety of transition words, phrases, and clauses to convey sequence and signal shifts from one time frame or setting to another.	**W.7.3c** Use a variety of transition words, phrases, and clauses to convey sequence and signal shifts from one time frame or setting to another.	**W.8.3c** Use a variety of transition words, phrases, and clauses to convey sequence, signal shifts from one time frame or setting to another, and show the relationships among experiences and events.	**Lesson 14:** Writing the Body of a Narrative
W.6.3d Use precise words and phrases, relevant descriptive details, and sensory language to convey experiences and events.	**W.7.3d** Use precise words and phrases, relevant descriptive details, and sensory language to capture the action and convey experiences and events.	**W.8.3d** Use precise words and phrases, relevant descriptive details, and sensory language to capture the action and convey experiences and events.	**Lesson 14:** Writing the Body of a Narrative
W.6.3e Provide a conclusion that follows from the narrated experiences or events.	**W.7.3e** Provide a conclusion that follows from and reflects on the narrated experiences or events.	**W.8.3e** Provide a conclusion that follows from and reflects on the narrated experiences or events.	**Lesson 15:** Writing a Strong Conclusion
W.6.4, W.7.4, W.8.4 Produce clear and coherent writing in which the development, organization, and style are appropriate to task, purpose, and audience.			**All lessons**

Common Core State Standards for Writing			Lesson
W.6.5 With some guidance and support from peers and adults, develop and strengthen writing as needed by planning, revising, editing, rewriting, or trying a new approach.	**W.7.5** With some guidance and support from peers and adults, develop and strengthen writing as needed by planning, revising, editing, rewriting, or trying a new approach, focusing on how well purpose and audience have been addressed.	**W.8.5** With some guidance and support from peers and adults, develop and strengthen writing as needed by planning, revising, editing, rewriting, or trying a new approach, focusing on how well purpose and audience have been addressed.	**Lesson 2:** Brainstorming **Lesson 3:** Jump-Starting Your Writing **Lesson 4:** Mapping Your Topic **Lesson 16:** Revising Your Writing
W.6.6 Use technology, including the Internet, to produce and publish writing as well as to interact and collaborate with others; demonstrate sufficient command of keyboarding skills to type a minimum of three pages in a single sitting.	**W.7.6** Use technology, including the Internet, to produce and publish writing and link to and cite sources as well as to interact and collaborate with others, including linking to and citing sources.	**W.8.6** Use technology, including the Internet, to produce and publish writing and present the relationships between information and ideas efficiently as well as to interact and collaborate with others.	**Lesson 30:** Seeing Your Work Out in the World
W.6.7 Conduct short research projects to answer a question, drawing on several sources and refocusing the inquiry when appropriate.	**W.7.7** Conduct short research projects to answer a question, drawing on several sources and generating additional related, focused questions for further research and investigation.	**W.8.7** Conduct short research projects to answer a question (including a self-generated question), drawing on several sources and generating additional related, focused questions that allow for multiple avenues of exploration.	**Lesson 6:** Researching Your Topic
W.6.8 Gather relevant information from multiple print and digital sources; assess the credibility of each source; and quote or paraphrase the data and conclusions of others while avoiding plagiarism and providing basic bibliographic information for sources.	**W.7.8** Gather relevant information from multiple print and digital sources, using search terms effectively; assess the credibility and accuracy of each source; and quote or paraphrase the data and conclusions of others while avoiding plagiarism and following a standard format for citation.	**W.8.8** Gather relevant information from multiple print and digital sources, using search terms effectively; assess the credibility and accuracy of each source; and quote or paraphrase the data and conclusions of others while avoiding plagiarism and following a standard format for citation.	**Lesson 6:** Researching Your Topic

Common Core State Standards for Writing	Lesson
W.6.9, W.7.9, W.8.9 Draw evidence from literary or informational texts to support analysis, reflection, and research.	**Lesson 5:** Defining and Developing Your Topic **Lesson 13:** Writing the Body Paragraphs
W.6.10, W.7.10, W.8.10 Write routinely over extended time frames (time for research, reflection, and revision) and shorter time frames (a single sitting or a day or two) for a range of discipline-specific tasks, purposes, and audiences.	**All lessons** **Lesson 10:** Planning for On-Demand Writing

Common Core State Standards for Language	Lesson
L.6.1 Demonstrate command of the conventions of standard English grammar and usage when writing or speaking.	**Lesson 19:** The Big Four Parts of Speech
L.6.1a Ensure that pronouns are in the proper case (subjective, objective, possessive).	**Lesson 21:** The All-Important Pronouns
L.6.1b Use intensive pronouns (e.g., *myself, ourselves*).	**Lesson 21:** The All-Important Pronouns
L.6.1c Recognize and correct inappropriate shifts in pronoun number and person.	**Lesson 27:** Avoiding Common Errors, Part 1
L.6.1d Recognize and correct vague pronouns (i.e., ones with unclear or ambiguous antecedents).	**Lesson 27:** Avoiding Common Errors, Part 1
L.6.1e Recognize variations from standard English in their own and others' writing and speaking, and identify and use strategies to improve expression in conventional language.	**Lesson 26:** Proofreading Your Writing **Lesson 27:** Avoiding Common Errors, Part 1 **Lesson 28:** Avoiding Common Errors, Part 2
L6.2 Demonstrate command of the conventions of standard English capitalization, punctuation, and spelling when writing.	Lessons 24, 25, and 26 as outlined below
L.6.2a Use punctuation (commas, parentheses, dashes) to set off nonrestrictive/parenthetical elements.	**Lesson 24:** Commas, Commas, Commas **Lesson 25:** Other Punctuation Marks
L.6.2b Spell correctly.	**Lesson 26:** Proofreading Your Writing
L6.3 Use knowledge of language and its conventions when writing, speaking, reading, or listening.	**Lesson 19:** The Big Four Parts of Speech
L.6.3a Vary sentence patterns for meaning, reader/listener interest, and style.	**Lesson 18:** Editing Your Writing: Habits to Adopt
L.6.3b Maintain consistency in style and tone.	**Lesson 17:** Editing Your Writing: Habits to Avoid
L.7.1 Demonstrate command of the conventions of standard English grammar and usage when writing or speaking.	**Lesson 19:** The Big Four Parts of Speech
L.7.1a Explain the function of phrases and clauses in general and their function in specific sentences.	**Lesson 22:** Verbals **Lesson 23:** Sentence Structure
L.7.1b Choose among simple, compound, complex, and compound-complex sentences to signal differing relationships among ideas.	**Lesson 23:** Sentence Structure
L.7.1c Place phrases and clauses within a sentence, recognizing and correcting misplaced and dangling modifiers.	**Lesson 28:** Avoiding Common Errors, Part 2
L.7.2 Demonstrate command of the conventions of standard English capitalization, punctuation, and spelling when writing.	Lessons 24 and 26 as outlined below
L.7.2a Use a comma to separate coordinate adjectives (e.g., *It was a fascinating, enjoyable movie* but not *He wore an old[,] green shirt*).	**Lesson 24:** Commas, Commas, Commas

Common Core State Standards for Language	Lesson
L.7.2b Spell correctly.	**Lesson 26:** Proofreading Your Writing
L.7.3 Use knowledge of language and its conventions when writing, speaking, reading, or listening.	**Lesson 19:** The Big Four Parts of Speech
L.7.3a Choose language that expresses ideas precisely and concisely, recognizing and eliminating wordiness and redundancy.	**Lesson 17:** Editing Your Writing: Habits to Avoid
L.8.1 Demonstrate command of the conventions of standard English grammar and usage when writing or speaking.	**Lesson 19:** The Big Four Parts of Speech
L.8.1a Explain the function of verbals (gerunds, participles, infinitives) in general and their function in particular sentences.	**Lesson 22:** Verbals
L.8.1b Form and use verbs in the active and passive voice.	**Lesson 20:** Properties of Verbs
L.8.1c Form and use verbs in the indicative, imperative, interrogative, conditional, and subjunctive mood.	**Lesson 20:** Properties of Verbs
L.8.1d Recognize and correct inappropriate shifts in verb voice and mood.	**Lesson 20:** Properties of Verbs **Lesson 27:** Avoiding Common Errors, Part 1
L.8.2 Demonstrate command of the conventions of standard English capitalization, punctuation, and spelling when writing.	Lessons 24, 25, and 26 as outlined below
L.8.2a Use punctuation (comma, ellipsis, dash) to indicate a pause or break.	**Lesson 24:** Commas, Commas, Commas **Lesson 25:** Other Punctuation Marks
L.8.2b Use an ellipsis to indicate an omission.	**Lesson 25:** Other Punctuation Marks
L.8.2c Spell correctly.	**Lesson 26:** Proofreading Your Writing
L.8.3 Use knowledge of language and its conventions when writing, speaking, reading, or listening.	**Lesson 19:** The Big Four Parts of Speech
L.8.3a Use verbs in the active and passive voice and in the conditional and subjunctive mood to achieve particular effects (e.g., emphasizing the actor or the action; expressing uncertainty or describing a state contrary to fact).	**Lesson 20:** Properties of Verbs

Pretest

Before you get started on the lessons, take this 30-question test. It will give you a sense of what you already know about writing and the writing process. Give yourself about 30 minutes for the test. Afterward, use the answer key to see how you did. The answer key tells you which lesson addresses the skill or concept that each question represents, so that you know which lessons might need more of your attention.

For questions 1–30, circle the letter next to your answer choice.

1. What is the final aim of prewriting?
   a. to overcome fears of writing
   b. to develop a plan for writing
   c. to determine what text type to write
   d. to write without worrying about details

2. Which of the following BEST defines the word *claim*?
   a. a belief that may or may not be true
   b. a reason to support an opinion or idea
   c. a statement of the author's point of view
   d. an idea the author wants readers to understand

3. What is the main purpose of writing an informational text?
   a. to share knowledge on a topic
   b. to persuade others to share your views
   c. to explain research you have done on a topic
   d. to tell about things that you know and others do not

4. What is the final aim of freewriting?
   a. to write a lot
   b. to have fun writing
   c. to put ideas in writing
   d. to forget about the rules

5. Which of the following is the BEST indicator of whether or not the information at a website is trustworthy?
   a. the credentials of the author
   b. the strength of its arguments
   c. the quality of the photography
   d. the number of links it provides

6. Which is the BEST thesis statement for an informational text on the topic of Pluto?
   a. Pluto is now said to be a "dwarf planet."
   b. Pluto used to be the ninth planet, but it is no longer.
   c. It's not really fair that Pluto isn't a planet anymore.
   d. Because of its size and location, Pluto is no longer called a planet.

7. What is the main purpose of writing an outline?
   a. to help you identify the thesis for your composition
   b. to ensure that your composition will be long enough
   c. to make a plan for each sentence in your composition
   d. to group and sequence information for your composition

8. Which organizational pattern do narratives tend to follow?
   a. spatial order
   b. cause and effect
   c. chronological order
   d. problem and solution

9. Which of the following is MOST LIKELY to help you write a successful response to an on-demand writing prompt?
   a. Use all of the available time to write your response.
   b. Take some time to plan, including planning your time.
   c. Spend the majority of the available time planning a response.
   d. Give at least half of your time to studying the prompt and other materials.

10. Which of the following is the BEST opening to an essay about *Little Women*, by Louisa May Alcott?
    a. Among my all-time favorite novels is *Little Women*, a classic by Louisa May Alcott.
    b. A century and a half after it was written, why do readers still enjoy *Little Women*, by Louisa May Alcott?
    c. *Little Women*, by Louisa May Alcott, is a novel about four sisters coming of age during and after the Civil War.
    d. In her novel *Little Women*, Louisa May Alcott gave lessons on how young women of her time should behave.

11. Which of the following BEST describes an effective introduction to an essay?
    a. It presents a clear and thorough thesis statement.
    b. It shocks or surprises readers so that they feel compelled to keep reading.
    c. It gives all background information that readers need to understand the topic.
    d. It engages readers and gives them a good sense of what the essay will be about.

12. Which of the following is likely to be the MOST convincing evidence to use in an argument?
    b. vivid descriptions
    a. personal anecdotes
    c. quotations from experts
    d. passionately felt reasons

13. What is the main purpose of using narrative techniques like description and dialogue?
   a. to bring an experience to life
   b. to display your skill as a writer
   c. to show differences between characters
   d. to make a fictional story from true events

14. Which practice can do the MOST to help you get new perspective on a draft you are planning to revise?
   a. Read it more slowly.
   b. Put it away for some time.
   c. Do some freewriting on your topic.
   d. Look at it carefully for small errors.

Read the following paragraph, and then answer questions 15–18 based on the paragraph.

> The Himalayas are the highest mountains in the world. They are also among the youngest. They started to form 40 or 50 million years ago. They got their start because India is smashing into Asia. They may have become the highest mountains on Earth only 600,000 years ago. They are still growing.

15. Which of the following changes would do the MOST to improve the beginning of this paragraph?
   a. Change "youngest" in the second sentence to "most youthful."
   b. Add a transition to the beginning of the second sentence: "Additionally, they are among the youngest."
   c. Combine the first two sentences: "The highest mountains in the world, the Himalayas are also among the youngest."
   d. No change

16. Which of the following sentences from the paragraph should be revised in order to maintain a formal tone?
   a. "They started to form 40 or 50 million years ago."
   b. "They got their start because India is smashing into Asia."
   c. "They may have become the highest mountains on Earth only 600,000 years ago."
   d. "They are still growing."

17. Which of the following would be the BEST transition word to add to the beginning of the final sentence of the paragraph?

    a. Thus . . .

    d. Similarly . . .

    c. Moreover . . .

    b. Nevertheless . . .

18. Which of the following domain-specific terms could be used to make the information in this paragraph more specific?

    a. *evolution*, having to do with changes to species over time

    b. *atmosphere*, having to do with the gasses that surround Earth

    c. *plate tectonics*, having to do with how continental plates move

    d. *cultural diversity*, having to do with the variety of human behaviors and beliefs

19. Which of the following sentences includes a clause in the conditional mood?

    a. Please, I said to go home!

    b. If I were you, I would leave now.

    c. I prefer to stay, but she wants to leave.

    d. Are you planning to stay here or go there?

20. In which of the following sentences is the underlined pronoun or pronouns used correctly?

    a. To <u>who</u> should I address this letter?

    b. My aunt invited <u>him and I</u> to go to the movies.

    c. You said that the best speller in the class is <u>whom</u>?

    d. The teacher told <u>her and me</u> to go to the whiteboard.

21. Which of the following sentences has a gerund as its subject?

    a. We'll stay indoors until it stops raining.

    b. The laughing child made us all laugh, too.

    c. Walking regularly can help to keep you healthy.

    d. Running along the river, she saw a fish leap out of the water.

22. Which of the following sentences is a complex sentence?
   a. When he said that, I laughed.
   b. After dinner, we went right to bed.
   c. I would call more often, but you never answer.
   d. Between my math and science classes, I have lunch.

23. In which of the following phrases is the comma used correctly?
   a. the red, woolen sweater
   b. the old, gardening tools
   c. the tall, handsome stranger
   d. the delicious, Italian meal

24. In which of the following sentences is punctuation BEST used to give emphasis to an idea?
   a. Tomorrow is my recital, my first.
   b. Tomorrow is my recital (my first).
   c. Tomorrow is my recital—my first!
   d. Tomorrow is my recital . . . my first.

25. Why should you not rely on spell-checking and grammar-checking programs?
   a. They are buggy and inconsistent.
   b. They are unable to identify all errors.
   c. Nearly all of the errors they identify are not actually problems.
   d. Using them keeps you from learning correct spelling and language use.

26. Read this sentence:

   Spaghetti and meatballs are my favorite meal.

Which of the following changes should be made to the sentence?
   a. Add a comma after "Spaghetti."
   b. Change "are" to "is."
   c. Change "my" to "mine."
   d. No change

27. Read this sentence:

What a mess! Nothing is in their place.

Which of the following changes should be made to the sentence?
a. Change "is" to "could be."
b. Change "their" to "its."
c. Change "place" to "places."
d. No change

28. Read this sentence:

The teacher demanded that the student return the stolen item and also apologizes.

Which of the following changes should be made to the sentence?
a. Change "demanded" to "would demand."
b. Change "return" to "returns."
c. Change "apologizes" to "apologize."
d. No change

29. Read this sentence:

I would like to go today, however my sister can't go until tomorrow.

Which of the following changes should be made to the sentence?
a. Change "however" to "but."
b. Add a comma after "however."
c. Change "go until tomorrow" to "go, not until tomorrow."
d. No change

30. Read this sentence:

Biking through the park this morning, the leaves were beginning to sprout.

Which of the following changes should be made to the sentence?
a. Change "Biking" to "While biking."
b. Change "the leaves were" to "I saw the leaves."
c. Add a comma after "park" and delete the comma after "morning."
d. No change

Answer Key

1. a. Sections 1 & 2
2. c. Lesson 1
3. a. Lesson 1
4. c. Lesson 3
5. a. Lesson 6
6. d. Lesson 7
7. d. Lesson 8
8. c. Lesson 9
9. b. Lesson 10
10. b. Lesson 11
11. d. Lesson 12
12. c. Lesson 13
13. a. Lesson 14
14. b. Lesson 16
15. c. Lesson 18
16. b. Lesson 17
17. c. Lesson 18
18. c. Lesson 18
19. b. Lesson 20
20. d. Lesson 21
21. c. Lesson 22
22. a. Lesson 23
23. c. Lesson 24
24. c. Lesson 25
25. b. Lesson 25
26. b. Lesson 27
27. b. Lesson 27
28. c. Lesson 27
29. a. Lesson 28
30. b. Lesson 28

Section 1

Getting Started

Even the most experienced writers frequently face the blank page with anxiety. Fortunately, there are a number of prewriting strategies that both experienced and less experienced writers can use to get started on a new project. **Prewriting** is a term that refers to the beginning stages of writing, when your focus is on generating ideas and outlining the general structure of your composition. In this section of the book, we'll focus on strategies that can help you come up with ideas before you sit down to write. Then in the next section, we'll look at strategies for planning the structure of your composition.

1

What's Your Purpose?

I'm happy to be a writer, of prose, poetry, every kind of writing. Every person in the world who isn't a recluse, hermit, or mute uses words. I know of no other art form that we always use.
—MAYA ANGELOU (1928–2014),
AMERICAN POET, AUTHOR, AND CIVIL-RIGHTS ACTIVIST

Understanding your purpose for writing is a crucial part of the writing process, beginning with prewriting. So, before we look at (and practice) prewriting strategies, let's review the purposes for writing—in other words, the reason to write in the first place. In this lesson, you'll learn about the goals for writing each of the three most common types of text: argument, informational text, and narrative. These are the text types identified in Anchor Standards for Writing 1, 2, and 3.

Do you write essays for school assignments? Do you write in a journal? Do you write emails or letters to family and friends?

If your answer to any of these questions is yes—and it almost certainly is—then guess what? You're a writer!

From middle-school students to Nobel Prize–winning novelists, writers of all kinds write for specific purposes. Your **purpose** is your reason for writing. For example, your purpose for writing an essay for a history class might be to demonstrate how much you understand a certain historical event. Your purpose for writing in a journal might be to work out your confusion about a misunderstanding between you and your best friend. Your purpose for writing an email to a family member might be to update him or her about what's going on in your life.

As you can see from these examples, there's a close relationship between your purpose as a writer and the type of text you create. Certain text types suit certain purposes. You're not likely to write an epic poem to thank your aunt for a birthday gift or write an essay to tell a friend about what you did on vacation.

In this lesson, we're going to look at three major text types: argument, informational text, and narrative. Most of your school assignments throughout middle school and beyond will take the form of one of these text types. Generally speaking, your main purpose for writing an argument, informational text, or narrative for school will be to fulfill the requirements of the assignment that your teacher gives you. However, if you're able to determine your own purpose for writing, too, you can make the assignment your own—and make your work stand out.

Arguments

Let's say that your purpose for writing is to persuade readers to take your point of view about a certain subject (for instance, that one sports team is more talented than another) or to convince them to take a particular action (for instance, vote for you to be class president). In both of these cases, your writing will take the form of an **argument**.

In an argument, you make a **claim**—in other words, you clearly state your point of view or opinion about a topic. Here are some examples of the claim you might make while writing an argument:

- **In an essay for an English class:** In Shakespeare's *Romeo and Juliet*, Romeo is in love with love more than he is with Juliet.

- **In an essay for a history class:** American society today would benefit if more people understood the phrase "the pursuit of happiness" in the way that Thomas Jefferson intended.

- **In an essay for a social studies class:** Violence in the movies is resulting in violence in our communities.

- **In an essay for a science class:** The results of our experiment show that the tap water in our town is a much better source of drinking water than any brand of bottled water.

- **In an editorial for your school paper:** Because of my commitment to improving our school for every member of the student body, I am the best candidate for the job of class president.

- **For your blog:** Save your money for the next update of *World of Wizardry*, because the current version of this video game is buggy and disappointing.

Unlike a face-to-face argument, a written argument may be passionate, but it doesn't involve shouting or verbally clobbering an opponent with your point of view. In fact, the readers of your argument aren't necessarily your opponents. They might be your teachers, classmates, or neighbors: people who may or may not agree with you, but who are willing to consider your perspective.

Therefore, in the most effective argument, you speak to your readers clearly, reasonably, and respectfully. To do so, you construct your claim precisely and support it with sound reasons and well-chosen evidence.

. . . .

TIP: Notice from this description of an effective argument that there's a close relationship between your purpose for writing, your audience, and your tone. The **audience** is the people whom you expect will be reading your work when you're done. The **tone** is the quality of your (or the narrator's) voice. If your purpose is to write an argument to persuade an audience of school officials to change a school rule, then you'll probably want to use a formal tone. If your purpose is to write a narrative to entertain an audience of your friends and classmates, you might want to use a casual, conversational tone.

. . . .

Informational Texts

If your purpose for writing is to inform or explain, then you'll write an **informational** or **expository text**. For example, you'll want to write an informational or expository text if you plan to:

- **describe a process,** such as how a star is formed.

- **explain how something works,** such as an internal combustion engine.

- **compare and contrast two or more ideas or things,** such as the U.S. Bill of Rights and the Universal Declaration of Human Rights.

- **explain a cause-and-effect relationship,** such as the way that burning fossil fuels can cause climate change.

- **define certain types or components of things,** such as the different families of primates or the elements of a sonnet.

As you can see from these examples, your job in writing an informational or expository text is to increase your reader's knowledge or understanding of a subject. To do so, you might provide examples, facts, and relevant anecdotes, as well as any personal knowledge you have on the subject.

There are some similarities between arguments and informational texts. For instance, a well-reasoned argument may include examples, facts, or relevant anecdotes as supporting evidence, too. But remember that the purpose of writing an argument is very different from the purpose of writing an informational text. In an argument, your goal is to persuade the reader to agree with your point of view. In an informational or explanatory text, your goal is simply to explain what, why, or how.

• •

TIP: Arguments and informational texts may be organized similarly and include similar types of information, but their purposes are different. The goal of an argument is to persuade. The goal of an informational or explanatory text is to explain what, why, or how.

• •

Narratives

If your purpose for writing is to tell a story or explore the significance of an event, then you'll write a **narrative**. Narratives tell about real or imagined experiences. Their organization is based on time (for example, the sequence in which events occur) and cause and effect (for example, how events affect characters or how they lead to other events).

Examples of narratives include the following:

- **novels,** such as *The Catcher in the Rye* and *A Tale of Two Cities*

- **short stories,** such as "The Tell-Tale Heart" and "Harrison Bergeron"

- **memoirs,** such as *I Know Why the Caged Bird Sings*

- **autobiographies,** such as *The Story of My Life*, by Helen Keller

- **biographies or accounts of historical events,** such as a writing assignment you might have for a history class

- **narrative accounts of investigations or procedures,** such as a writing assignment you might have for a science class

Whether you're writing from experience or from your imagination, you generally have two main jobs when creating a narrative. (These jobs may not apply, however, to more formal types of narratives, such as an account of a scientific investigation.) Your first job is to make the experience come alive for your readers. To do so, you use such narrative techniques as dialogue and sensory detail. Your second job is to reveal the significance of the experience, which may be done directly, through reflection, or indirectly, through the implications of the plot, imagery, or other elements of the narrative.

· ·

TIP: The 16th-century French writer Michel de Montaigne was the first author to use the word *essays* (or, in French, *essais*) to describe his writing. This word means "attempt" or "trial," and it described his meandering style well. Now, however, we often use the word *essay* when we are talking about a different sort of writing.

In this book, we will use the word **essay** to refer to a piece of writing that states a main idea, supports that idea, and builds to a conclusion. Arguments and informational texts typically take this form, but narratives often do not. We will use the word **composition** to refer to any piece of writing—argument, informational text, or narrative.

Other Forms of Writing

The argument, informational text, and narrative aren't the only forms of writing. They aren't even likely to be the only forms of writing that you'll do in middle school and afterward. Some other types of writing are described below.

- The **response to literature** is a specific kind of argument in which you share your understanding of one or more works of literature. In your response, you might tell about your interpretation of the work or works. You might also tell about your critical view, or evaluation, of the work or works.

- A **research paper** may offer an analysis of a subject, or it may present an argument. Either way, the author of a successful research paper takes up a question, investigates primary and secondary sources in order to answer the question, and then writes up his or her findings in a thoughtful, well-organized paper. See Lesson 6 for more information about doing research.

- For your state test or an admissions test like the SAT, you may be asked to write on demand in **response to a prompt**. A **prompt** is a question or assignment intended to elicit a particular kind of response. The response can take many forms. You might be asked to argue in response to a question, for example, or you might be asked to tell about and reflect on an experience. See Lesson 10 for guidance on this kind of writing.

- **Poetry** is a form that reflects the poet's special care with language. Much contemporary poetry is lyric, expressing the experience and feelings of a first-person speaker. However, poetry may also be written in dramatic or narrative modes.

- **Drama** is written for performance, usually by actors in a theater.

- **Journaling** is a personal and often private form of writing, in which the author tells about and reflects on his or her observations and experiences. The committed journal keeper writes regularly—often daily. See Lesson 3 for more thoughts about journaling.

- **Letters** take many forms, including thank-you notes, updates between family or friends, and business correspondence. Although you might tend to keep in touch through email, text messages, and posts on social media, the letter remains a useful form to learn.

Practice 1: Setting Your Purpose

There are many ways to approach the same topic in writing. The approach you choose, as you've seen, depends on your purpose.

Let's consider the topic of the first day of school—your own first day of school (in kindergarten, earlier this year, or whenever) or someone else's. What kind of argument might you write on this topic? What kind of informational text or narrative might you write?

Define a purpose for writing about this topic that matches each text type below. Identify the intended audience and an appropriate tone (for example, formal, casual, etc.). Then write an engaging first sentence for each text type.

Text Type	Purpose for Writing	Audience	Tone	First Sentence
Argument				
Informational text				
Narrative				

2

Brainstorming

Inspiration is wonderful when it happens, but the writer must develop an approach for the rest of the time.
—LEONARD BERNSTEIN (1918–1990),
AMERICAN COMPOSER AND CONDUCTOR

In this lesson, you'll learn about brainstorming, a prewriting strategy that is one of the best ways to get your brain—and your pen—started on an assignment. You can use brainstorming to help you develop a plan for any type of writing, from a poem to an article for your school newspaper. Planning is the first step of the writing process outlined in Anchor Standard for Writing 5.

For many, facing the blank page is the most difficult part of a writing assignment. If you happen to be one of those people who dread getting started, remembering the following three things just might ease the pressure:

1. Writing is a process. In this book, we'll be walking you through the writing process, which includes prewriting, drafting, revising, and editing. Each of these stages gives you another opportunity to generate and further refine your ideas and language. Therefore,

you don't have to get it right (whatever "right" might be) the first time, nor even the second, third, or fourth time.

2. There are many low-pressure ways to start filling the page with words. We'll give you some ideas on how to do so in this and the next two lessons. In this lesson, we'll start with brainstorming.

3. And hey, if the worst part of the writing process for you is getting started, then the good news is that once you've begun, you've already overcome the hardest part of getting the assignment done!

What Is Brainstorming?

Believe it or not, the word *brainstorm* originally referred to a state of mental confusion or disturbance. Then, in the mid-20th century, it came to be used as a verb to refer to a specific type of group activity. In this kind of brainstorming, a group of people work together to come up with new ideas or find a creative solution to a problem. Each person throws out as many ideas as come to mind, and everyone's ideas are recorded—even those ideas that seem outlandish or otherwise off-the-mark. In fact, group members are encouraged to build on others' ideas rather than evaluate or criticize them.

Now the word **brainstorming** refers to any process of generating ideas without criticizing or filtering them. You can brainstorm with a group, or you can brainstorm on your own. It's a great way to get started writing. Because when you're brainstorming, even your silliest ideas are worth writing down! Doesn't that take the pressure off?

The Benefits of Brainstorming

Brainstorming can help you come up with ideas any time you have a writing assignment or another occasion for writing.

When you have a writing assignment, your teacher will probably provide guidelines about the form that your writing should take—a research paper or response to literature, for example—as well as a general topic or question. These guidelines provide you with a starting point, and you can brainstorm in order to explore the writing topic or consider answers to the question. If the assignment allows you to choose a topic, then you can take some time to brainstorm about each possible topic to help you decide which one to write about. The topic that stimulates the most ideas immediately is most likely the one that interests you most.

Not every occasion for writing begins with an assignment or guidelines, though. There are no set guidelines for writing in your journal or writing for your blog, for example—unless you've made your own rules. When you're writing without guidelines, brainstorming can help you shape your writing. As when you're writing for an assignment, you can brainstorm in order to find a topic (if you don't already have one), as well as to discover what you want to say about the topic.

The Brainstorming Process

When you're brainstorming, you don't need to do anything more complicated than list your ideas as they come to you. Don't worry about spelling, punctuation, or writing in complete sentences. How's that for low pressure?

Here's the process you can follow:

1. Establish a time limit for yourself. If you have just 30 minutes to write for a timed assignment, your brainstorming session might be as short as 3 minutes long. Or if you have a week or two to work on a school assignment, you might brainstorm for 30 minutes one day and another 30 minutes a day later, after your ideas have simmered overnight.
2. Write your topic or question at the top of the page, and then write down ideas as quickly as you can. Jot down whatever comes to you—individual words, phrases, questions—and don't worry about their making sense or appearing in order.
3. Once your allotted time is up, take a deep breath, and try to clear your brain. If you have the time to do so, go out for a walk or get up and jog in place for a few minutes to activate your energy.
4. Now look over and consider the ideas you've written down. Cross out the ideas that strike you as unworkable, and underline or circle the words, phrases, and ideas that strike a chord in your mind. If related or additional ideas come to you, add them to your list.
5. Among your jottings you are likely to find something that appeals to you as a potential main topic or central idea. Spend some more time brainstorming about this topic or idea, to help you refine it further and understand your particular point of view on it.

Brainstorming Triggers

A **trigger** is something that stimulates an action or reaction. In the context of writing, a trigger is something that stimulates writing. Effective triggers include the following:

- **Sentence starters,** such as "I remember . . ." (for generating ideas for a personal essay) or "My topic is like . . ." (for generating similes that can help you view your topic creatively) or simply "I want to know . . ." (for generating ideas for a research paper)

- **The six questions** a journalist tries to answer: Who? What? Where? When? Why? How?

- **The five senses,** which you can focus on using questions such as "What smells [or sounds, or textures, etc.] do I remember from that time?" (for generating ideas for a personal essay) or "What sights [or sounds, or tastes, etc.] are related to this topic?"

. . . .

TIP: Keep the *storm* in *brainstorm* in mind as you brainstorm. Storms are chaotic and leave messes behind. So don't hold back or worry about how strange or messy your writing might get while you're brainstorming. Once you've made your ideas concrete by writing them down, it'll be that much easier to organize and make sense out of them later.

. . . .

A Sample of Brainstorming on a Topic

Here's a sample of what one student wrote while brainstorming on the topic of global warming. Her science teacher had given this general topic in an assignment for writing an informational text. Her purpose for brainstorming was to list the aspects of the topic that interested her, so that she could choose a specific topic for her informational text. Notice that her list includes many questions about the topic; such questions often suggest avenues for further exploration.

GLOBAL WARMING

Big issue in politics—is it Democrats or Republicans who will fix it more?

Future generations will suffer. How fast is it happening?

Polar bears are dying out because of ice caps melting

What about other animals? seals, sharks, dolphins?

Fumes from cars are causing earth to heat up

Factories—are they the cause of it? What about little countries like Peru?

How much is due to China being so important nowadays?

Last summer was hottest summer we've had—even my uncle's corn crop got ruined

Atmosphere has a hole in it. (I don't really know what this means)

My dad's complaint about his fishing being affected . . . no more salmon in the river

Define global anyway. What does it really mean? Is the weather only world feature changing? Is the soil drying up? What about the oceans?

In the end, this student decided to write about the effects of global warming on polar bears. What else could have been an engaging topic for her informational text, given what she wrote while brainstorming? For example, she could have decided to use her father's fishing experiences as the starting point for a discussion of the local effects of global patterns, which may have resulted in a more personal essay. Or she could have chosen to write about the effects of global warming on a particular country; her question about Peru (and other smaller countries) suggests that she has some interest in or information about that country.

Do you see how useful brainstorming can be in helping you find a topic for writing? You can also brainstorm to generate ideas about what you want to say about your topic after you've chosen it. Remember, there really aren't any rights or wrongs in brainstorming. Its purpose is just to get your mind juiced up and working.

Practice 1: Practicing Brainstorming

Imagine that you've been given an assignment to write an argument on one of the following topics for your social studies class. Take five minutes to brainstorm on one of these topics.

Topic 1: The importance of social activities to students' learning

Topic 2: The Internet as the most powerful medium in the world today

Topic 3: The uses (and misuses) of computers as teaching devices in schools

Afterward, look over and consider the ideas you've written down. Which idea seems most appealing to you as the focus for your imagined argument? Circle it. What would be the central claim for your argument? Write it down.

_____

_____

_____

_____

_____

_____

_____

_____

_____

_____

_____

_____

3

Jump-Starting Your Writing

I write entirely to find out what I'm thinking, what I'm looking at, what I see and what it means. What I want and what I fear.
—JOAN DIDION (1934–),
AMERICAN NOVELIST AND ESSAYIST

In this lesson, you'll learn about freewriting, another prewriting strategy that can help you get started on an assignment. Prewriting, or planning your writing, is the first step of the writing process outlined in Anchor Standard for Writing 5.

Writing an essay or narrative might seem as challenging—and exhausting—as running a marathon. And like runners before a race, writers often warm up. Writers don't generally stretch or jog before writing, however (though doing so could be helpful). Instead, they warm up through practice writing sessions called freewriting.

What Is Freewriting?

Freewriting is the practice of writing continuously, usually in a timed session (as brief as five minutes or as long as an hour), without stopping to correct your spelling, language use, or sentence structure. If you get stuck and can't think of anything else to write, then you keep writing by writing about being stuck and having no ideas ("I am stuck and can't think of anything else to write . . . I am stuck, but now I notice how I'm feeling about . . ."). In fact, freewriting can be understood as the written form of idle thinking, the kind of mind wandering you do when you're on the bus, waiting to fall asleep, or trying not to pay attention to the dull conversation of the adults in the room with you.

Many writers find that it's easiest to begin freewriting with a topic in mind, no matter how simple, general, or vague. Once you've started writing, you can let your mind and your hand take you anywhere. Don't worry about staying on topic. You might even find yourself discovering ideas and connections you wouldn't have come to had you been using a more focused prewriting strategy.

Here's a sample of freewriting done by a student preparing to write a personal essay on the influence of television on his life, a topic assigned by his teacher. Note that the freewriting occasionally veers off the subject, but that when it does so, the student comes upon ideas that he may be able use to make relevant points and give specific examples in the essay he will write.

TELEVISION IN MY LIFE

I am really stuck trying to think of what to write about this topic, because television is a really important part of everybody life. Think of the war, we see it everyday on tv and then there are elections and politics and the goverrrment and the topic seems so big that I think the teacher wants to bad mouth television because she is always trying to get us to read books instead of watching tv so I thitkn this assignment is mostly to get us to say that we watch too mcuh television. The influence of television is really great, that's for sure. Think of how we get out news I don't read the papers and my parents don't even subscribe to a newspaper because when they did the papers would just pile up and no one had time in busy lifes to sit down and read all that detailed stuff that was not so important really and that is another reason that tv is very important because it becomes a way for all of us to learn things that we wouldn't kno if we dindt watch tv. And theirs also the entertainment factor. Plus babysitting. When I was little me and my brother watchd sesame street and I can remember even lerning stuff from that show that I still know. So maybe what I should write about is all the good things from tv and not try to suck up to the teacher and say that ttv is bad for us cause I think that is what she wants to hear in this paper.

- -

TIP: Whether you freewrite with pen and paper or on the computer is up to you. If you are more fluent when writing by hand, then write by hand. If you are more comfortable with a keyboard, then use a computer.

However, if you prefer the computer but don't already know how to touch type, now is the time to learn! Touch typing is the practice of using the home keys on your keyboard (*asdf* and *jkl;*) to type quickly without looking down. Being able to type quickly will help you write with more ease, because you will be less likely to lose your train of thought while you're hunting and pecking.

- -

On Keeping a List of Writing Topics

Having a personal list of potential writing topics for freewriting can be helpful, especially if you keep a journal, blog regularly, or are a budding writer of poems, stories, or personal essays. Here are a few potential writing topics to get you started with your own list:

- Tell about the funniest thing that you have experienced recently. As you tell what happened, remember the six questions a journalist tries to answer: Who? What? Where? When? Why? How?

- Describe your morning routine.

- Describe your favorite activity, and explain what it takes to get good at doing this activity.

- Describe your favorite place, doing your best to appeal to all five senses in telling about the place.

- Note an interesting line of poetry, sentence from a story or novel, or something you've heard someone say to you or someone else. (Great writers are often great eavesdroppers!) Use this line, sentence, or bit of dialogue to get your freewriting started.

For an extended list of potential writing topics, as well as wonderful insight into the writing process, see the book *Writing Down the Bones*, by Natalie Goldberg, a classic work about freewriting and the writing life.

On Keeping a Journal

One writing practice that is a close relative of freewriting is that of keeping a journal. In a journal, you may freewrite, or you may write quickly, but with a little more conscious attention than one usually gives to freewriting. Either way, many writers, artists, and scientists (neurologist Oliver Sacks filled nearly a thousand volumes in his lifetime) find that writing a little (or a lot) every day helps them in numerous ways.

- Journaling provides a place to record private thoughts that the writer doesn't feel comfortable sharing with others.

- Journaling is often prescribed by doctors who find that writing helps people get through physical or emotional problems they are experiencing.

- Journaling is a good way to vent. Better to yell at someone in your private journal than to yell at them in person.

- Journaling helps writers improve their craft. "Practice makes perfect," just as your mother may have told you.

- Journaling provides a good place for warehousing an inventory of ideas you'd like to write about someday. This is perhaps the most common writer's use of journaling. Ideas for future poems, stories, and essays can be recorded in the journal and kept there for future reference and development.

Practice 1: Practicing Freewriting

Now try freewriting on your own. Choose one of the writing topics listed on page 30, set a timer for five minutes, and go! You may write on this page, on a separate piece of paper, or on your computer. Choose the place that will encourage you to write most freely.

_____

_____

_____

_____

_____

_____

_____

_____

_____

_____

_____

_____

_____

_____

_____

_____

_____

_____

_____

_____

_____

_____

4

Mapping Your Topic

Writing is like walking in a deserted street.
Out of the dust in the street you make a mud pie.
—JOHN LE CARRÉ (1931–),
BRITISH SPY NOVELIST

In this lesson, you'll learn another prewriting strategy. This strategy helps you discover relationships between your ideas as you plan your writing. Planning is the first step of the writing process outlined in Anchor Standard for Writing 5.

Maybe you're a visual thinker—that is, you tend to think in terms of pictures or images. Or maybe you're a nonlinear thinker—that is, your ideas tend to come to you in clusters rather than seeming to line up one after the other. If so, you might find that creating an idea web is an especially effective approach to prewriting.

What Is an Idea Web?

An **idea web** shows the relationships between different ideas. An idea web might show these relationships in a decentralized web. Or it might show relationships as hierarchical, with ideas branching off from a central concept. Here is an example of an idea web, created by a student planning an informational text on environmental issues in his town.

Local Environmental Issues

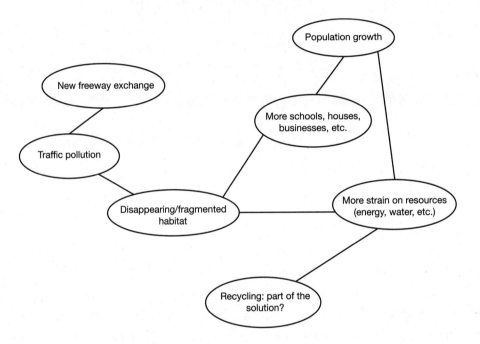

There are two main ways to create an idea web.

Write First, Make the Web Later

One way to make an idea web is to write down your ideas first and find the relationships among them afterward. Write your ideas as they come to you, spreading them all over the page. Circle each individual idea. Once you've filled the page, sit back and consider your ideas. As you find relationships among the ideas, connect them with lines or arrows. You might also cross out ideas that don't really contribute to the network of relationships that emerges as you create the idea web. (The idea web pictured above was created in this way.)

Web as You Go

Another way to make an idea web is to focus on relationships as you write down your ideas rather than afterward. Start by writing one central theme or the general topic at the center of the page. Draw spokes radiating from this general idea, and write a closely related idea at the end of each spoke. Then draw spokes from each of those ideas, and write any related ideas or specific examples at the end of those spokes. Continue branching until you fill the page or run out of ideas.

Here is an example of an idea web created in this way, representing the same ideas on local environmental issues as on the idea web above. Notice that on this idea web, ideas are arranged in a hierarchy, with the general topic at the center of the web and supporting ideas and details branching out from it.

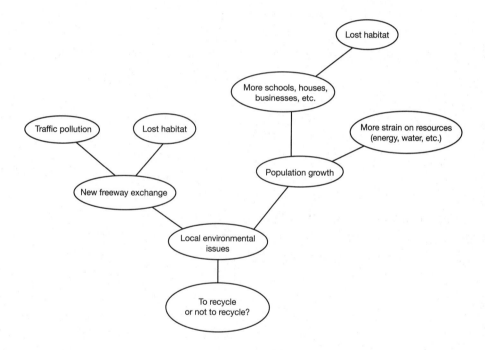

You might not think in such an orderly way, and your maps might not look so tidy, which is perfectly all right. What's important is to get lots of ideas down on paper. And even by making the least tidy idea web, you're starting to bring some order to your ideas. That will be your next step in prewriting: to organize your ideas.

· ·

TIP: Prewriting strategies such as brainstorming, freewriting, and creating idea webs are great ways to generate ideas when you're not sure what to write about, particularly when you fear that you have nothing to say about an assigned topic. But note that these are also great ways to focus your thinking when you fear that you have *too much* to say about an assigned topic. A way of organizing your ideas might emerge. Or a specific focus for your writing might become clear.

For example, notice that in the example idea webs, the specific topics of strained resources and lost habitat connect to many other ideas or are repeated. One or the other of these specific topics is therefore likely to be a good focus for the student's informational text.

· ·

Practice 1: Write First, Make the Web Later

In Lesson 1, you generated ideas about an argument, informational text, and narrative that you could write on the topic of the first day of school. Imagine that you want to take the next step and develop one of these projects.

Choose one of the ideas you came up with for Lesson 1, and set a timer for three minutes. On a separate sheet of paper, write down all of the ideas you could use in this piece of writing. Spread your ideas all over the page, and circle each individual idea. When your time is up, consider your ideas and connect them with lines or arrows. Cross out any that don't seem promising. Remember, there are no right or wrong answers!

Practice 2: Web as You Go

On another sheet of paper, create an idea web for a personal essay on the topic of "my wish for the future." This time, start by writing this topic at the center of a sheet of paper. Set a timer for three minutes, and go! First, write specific ideas that relate to this general topic, and then, radiating from those ideas, write any related ideas or specific examples. Continue branching until your time is up.

After you complete this second idea web, reflect on your work. Which approach to mapping your topic do you prefer?

Section 2

Planning Your Writing

In the previous section, we focused on the first step of prewriting: to generate ideas and get them down on paper (or your word processor). Now, we'll focus on the next step: to organize these ideas and make a plan.

The fact that writers need to plan their writing shouldn't come as a surprise. After all, every task needs a plan, even a simple one. For example, think about what you do every morning to get ready for your day. How many steps are involved? Do you do them in the same order every day? Why do you do them in that order? The answer to the last question probably is: because this is the order that makes sense. (It wouldn't make sense to put your shoes on and then put your socks on!) Similarly, a writer needs to put her ideas in an order that makes sense—and before she does, she needs to come up with a plan for how she's going to do that. In this section, we'll look at strategies for evaluating your ideas and figuring out the best way to order them in your writing.

5

Defining and Developing Your Topic

This is what I learned: that everybody is talented, original and has something important to say.
—BRENDA UELAND (1891–1985),
AMERICAN WRITER, EDITOR, AND TEACHER

This lesson provides you with ways to select a specific topic and develop what you have to say about it. Whether or not you're writing for an assignment, you'll need to do some work both to focus your thinking and to make sure you have the information and details to support your central ideas. This work is essential to the planning stage of writing—the first step of the writing process outlined in Anchor Standard for Writing 5. Additionally, supporting and developing your ideas is the focus of Standards **W.6.1b, W.6.2b, W.6.3b, W.6.9, W.7.1b, W.7.2b, W.7.3b, W.7.9, W.8.1b, W.8.2b, W.8.3b**, and **W.8.9**.

So far you've read about and practiced several techniques to get you started writing, including brainstorming, freewriting, and creating idea webs. In applying these techniques, you might generate many words and ideas—many more than you can include in one composition. Before you can proceed, you need to decide on a focus for your writing. Once you decide on a specific topic, you will likely need to develop it further, through additional prewriting activities and research.

Defining Your Topic

If you've done some prewriting on your topic, you may already have decided on a focus for your writing. If you haven't done any prewriting yet, then what are you waiting for? (Review the previous section of this book to learn different ways to get started.) If you've done some prewriting but *aren't* yet sure of your focus, then review your brainstorming, freewriting, and/or idea webs and ask yourself the following questions:

- **Which ideas do I seem to have the most to say about?** Even when you're required to write within strict guidelines for a school assignment, try to focus on an aspect of the assignment that interests you the most. You'll do your best writing if you're genuinely engaged with your subject.

- **Which ideas am I most curious about?** Your prewriting may include several questions. Or there may be ideas in your prewriting that you don't yet have much to say about but that intrigue you. If you have the necessary time to put the thought and research needed to explore unfamiliar ideas, then why not go for it?

- **Which ideas best suit the purpose of the assignment?** Your personal recollections of your elementary school music program may interest you more than anything else, but they might not have any place (or only a supporting place) in your writing if you've been asked to write an argument about the role of the arts in public education.

- **Which ideas seem most appropriate for my audience?** Remember that the purpose of your writing is to communicate with an audience. You might be excited about a little-known aspect of gaming culture, but if you are writing for an audience that doesn't know much about video games, a more general approach is probably better.

Writing a Working Thesis Statement

The **thesis statement** presents the central idea or claim that you intend to support in an essay. It is usually one sentence (sometimes two) and appears in the introduction of your essay. At this point, you may not have a complete thesis statement in mind, but that's O.K. A working thesis statement can help guide your thinking.

A **working thesis statement** is temporary. It may be incomplete or even badly written. It doesn't need to be eloquent, but it does need to state your central idea, at least as you see it at this point. For example, let's say an assignment asks students to write an informational text in response to the question *What is the status of recycling efforts in our community today?* A student's working thesis might be the following:

> *The status of recycling efforts in our community today is not great.*

This thesis would not be specific enough for a final draft. But for now, it's good enough to suggest a focus for the informational text. As the student develops the topic, she'll need to find specific information and details to show exactly how and why recycling in her community is "not great."

Practice 1: Defining an Essay Topic

Look back at the brainstorming you did for practice in Lesson 2. At the time, you selected a focus and wrote a central claim for an argument. Now review what you wrote, using the questions listed above. Based on these questions, what focus would you now choose? (You might choose the same one as before, or you might not.) Would the central claim that you previously wrote serve as a good working thesis statement? If not, revise or replace it.

Developing Your Topic

Once you decide on a focus for your writing, take a look at your brainstorming, freewriting, and/or idea webs again. This time, review your prewriting in order to collect all of the ideas, examples, and questions that are relevant to the specific topic you have chosen. You could collect them in an organized list, in which you group related ideas, examples, and questions in categories. Or you could organize them in an idea web.

After you sift through your ideas, examine them again to see which ideas may need more development or support. You'll need different kinds of supporting ideas, information, and details, depending on the type of text you are writing. (For more information on these ways of supporting and developing your ideas, see Lesson 13.)

If you are writing an argument, then you need evidence that shows why your claim is valid, or true, such as . . .

- logical and compelling reasons
- specific examples, concrete details, and other types of facts that support your reasons
- anecdotes and descriptions
- quotations from experts about the issue
- quotations from people affected by the issue
- details about opposing views, and responses to these views

If you are writing a response to literature, then you need evidence that shows why your explanation of the text is valid, or true, such as . . .

- specific examples from the text
- anecdotes and descriptions
- quotations from the text
- quotations from other readers of the text

If you are writing an informational text, then you need information that helps readers understand your topic, such as . . .

- facts and definitions
- specific examples and concrete details
- anecdotes and descriptions
- quotations

If you are writing a narrative, then you need details that will develop the story and bring it to life, such as . . .

- sensory details and descriptions
- vividly drawn characters and events
- dialogue

You can do some additional brainstorming or freewriting to develop any ideas that need more support or development. You can also do some more thoughtful, deliberate writing; although even if you're not writing off the top of your head (as when you are freewriting), there's still no need to worry about spelling, punctuation, or language use. You can simply list the information, details, and quotations you plan to use.

You might also find that you need to do some research. That's the topic of the next lesson.

. . . .

TIP: At this stage of the writing process, you may begin to see why the writing process is often compared to an accordion. An accordion makes music as it expands and contracts. Similarly, as you work on a piece of writing, it may expand and contract several times as you alternate between developing your ideas and focusing them.

. . . .

Practice 2: Developing an Essay Topic

Here is the organized list made by a student whose working thesis in response to the question *What is the status of recycling efforts in our community today?* is *The status of recycling efforts in our community today is not great.*

Recycling in our community = not great.

1. People aren't recycling.
   - Collection bins are hard to get.
   - People don't understand what can/can't be recycled.
   - Do people even understand or care why recycling matters? I don't know.
   - Are people thinking that if no one else is recycling, why should they make the effort?

2. Poor leadership
   - There were a few newspaper articles when the recycling program started, but not much information has been shared since then.
   - It's not clear whether or not recycling is even happening at town offices or public schools.

Which ideas need more development or support? Circle them. Write down what kind of additional support is needed, and note any ideas you might have about where and how this support could be found.

6

Researching Your Topic

The greatest part of a writer's time is spent in reading, in order to write; a man will turn over half a library to make one book.
—SAMUEL JOHNSON (1709–1784),
ENGLISH WRITER

This lesson gives an overview of research methods and resources. Standards **W6.7**, **W6.8**, **W7.7**, **W7.8**, **W8.7**, and **W8.8** focus on the research process.

Research is the process of investigating a subject or question. You might do research to find the facts and examples to support your claim in an argument or to bring the topic of an informational text to life. You might even do research to help you write a narrative. For example, if you're writing a science fiction story set in an imagined desert, you might read about or examine photographs of actual deserts to give you ideas about how to make the setting of your story vivid and realistic.

No matter what your reason is for doing research, you should aim to bring thought and imagination to the process. In fact, the research process can be as creative as the writing process.

Library Research

The obvious place to start is with the print and electronic resources available at your library. Ask a reference librarian there for help finding or evaluating resources. Don't be afraid to ask! It's his or her job to help people find the books and information they need.

- **Reference works such as encyclopedias** provide general information on a wide variety of topics. Your library likely has one or more encyclopedias on its shelves and may also have access to encyclopedias online. A good encyclopedia article on your topic is likely to suggest additional questions about your topic.

- **Some nonfiction books** give an overview of a topic. Other nonfiction books examine just one aspect of a topic. A biography is a nonfiction book that tells about the life of a person.

- **Periodicals such as newspapers and magazines** offer up-to-date news or information on a topic. Your library likely has back issues of magazines. Your library likely can also give you access to online databases of newspaper and magazine articles.

- The **websites** of organizations related to your topic may provide useful information. For example, the Cornell Lab of Ornithology maintains an excellent guide to birds and bird watching (All About Birds) at its website. Similarly, Plimoth Plantation (a museum) maintains extensive information about early colonial New England at its website. Be especially cautious when using the Internet for your research. Many websites do not give valid information. See below for more information on deciding whether or not to use a website.

- For some research projects, **photographs, maps, and other graphic sources** may be useful. One place to search for images is the Prints and Photographs Online Catalog of the Library of Congress. This catalogue provides images from collections held by the Library of Congress.

- **Primary resources such as diaries, letters, and interviews** can provide a perspective on events from the time when they happened.

To check whether or not you should trust the information you get from a website, ask yourself the following questions:

- What is the purpose of the website? Is its main purpose to provide facts or to express opinions? Is it sponsored by a reputable organization (such as a school or government organization), or is it a personal website?

- Who is the author of the website? Does the author have a background that is relevant to the topic?

- Is the website well designed? Is the tone of the website calm and serious? Is it free of errors in grammar and spelling?

- How up-to-date is the information provided by the website?

- Do other trustworthy sites link to the website? Does the website link to trustworthy, up-to-date sites?

Be sure to keep clear and detailed records of the sources you use, so that you can provide a bibliography with your final essay. In particular, carefully note when you've quoted exact words or paraphrased from a source. You'll need to cite the source if you use this language in your final essay.

Keywords

Whether you're using a search engine or looking through the index of a book, identifying effective keywords is crucial for finding the information you need. **Keywords** are terms that identify important ideas related to a research topic or question. The best keywords name specific and relevant people, places, events, and concepts.

Let's say that the student writing about recycling efforts in her community wants to find information on successful recycling programs. The keywords she might use for an online search are *successful recycling programs examples*.

Practice 1: Identifying Keywords

Identify keywords that you could use to find information that helps you answer each of the following research questions. Then try out the keywords in a search engine to test their effectiveness!

Research questions	Keywords
During what periods of time has immigration to the United States been greatest?	
What are the main characteristics of a fairy tale?	
What made the flu so deadly in 1918?	

Creative Research

Different sources will reflect different elements of—and biases on—a subject. Therefore, it's best to draw from several sources as you perform your research. And you certainly don't need to limit yourself to library resources!

Consider the following possible research ideas:

- Set up an interview with at least one authority on your subject. This authority doesn't have to be the most important person with insight or influence on your topic. It could be your principal, a local official or community leader, a neighbor or grandparent with personal memories of an event, or a parent (yours or a classmate's) with expertise on the subject. Just get on the phone (or email) and ask! Someone just might agree to talk to you, especially if you made a good case for why you want to meet this person and how your interview could benefit both of you.

- Think creatively. For example, the student writing about recycling efforts in her community might talk to the manager of a nearby recycling plant—a person who may not be a community member but who almost certainly has valuable insight to offer.

- Generate your own data by conducting a survey or running an experiment.

. . . .

TIP: Like the writing process, the research process could be compared to an accordion. Your research might lead you toward additional questions on your topic. And one of these questions might turn out to be the best focus for your writing—which might in turn lead you toward additional questions. One key to doing research, then, is to know when to stop! If you've found what you need for your writing project, then start writing.

. . . .

Practice 2: Creative Research Ideas

Look back at Practice 2 in the previous lesson and see what additional information you identified as needed for the essay on recycling efforts.

What are two library resources that the student writing on this topic might find helpful?

1. _____

2. _____

What are two creative approaches to research that the student writing on this topic might find helpful?

1. _____

2. _____

7

Defining and Developing Your Thesis

Have common sense and stick to the point.
—W. Somerset Maugham (1874–1965),
British novelist

This lesson walks you through the process of developing a thesis statement or claim. Introducing your claim, topic, or point of view is one focus of Standards **W.6.1a**, W.6.2a, W.6.3a, W.7.1a, W.7.2a, W.7.3a, W.8.1a, W.8.2a, and **W.8.3a**.

In Lesson 5, you wrote a working thesis statement. In this lesson, you'll learn how to develop and refine your thesis statement. Remember, a thesis statement presents the central idea or claim that you intend to support in an essay.

A Three-Step Process for Developing Your Thesis Statement

To tell the truth, any thesis statement that you write at this point is still a working thesis. But even a working thesis can guide you as you write the first draft of an essay. And then, after you write that first draft, you can refine your thesis statement further, if necessary.

Here are three steps you can take to develop a clear, well-focused thesis statement.

Review the Assignment

If you're writing for a school assignment, reread the assignment. Writing a thesis statement might be as simple as drafting an answer to the question asked in the assignment. For example, remember the assignment that asks students to write an informational text in response to the question *What is the status of recycling efforts in our community today?* An answer to this question might be the following:

> *Most people in our community do not recycle items that can be recycled.*

Beware: student writers frequently make the mistake of straying away from the assignment and failing to fulfill its requirements. So don't skip this step! Always take another look at the guidelines for the assignment and check to make sure you haven't forgotten anything that relates to your thesis.

For example, if the assignment requires you to avoid stating personal opinions, then you know that a thesis statement like *I think it's a shame that more people in our community do not recycle* needs to be revised to eliminate the use of the first-person, "I." Or if the assignment asks you to write an informational text, then you know that a thesis statement like *We all need to make a better effort to recycle those things that can be recycled* needs to be revised, because it is more suitable for an argument than an informational text.

Finally, another aspect of the assignment that affects your thesis statement is the required length of the essay. A 500-word essay needs a much more narrowly focused thesis than a 10-page research paper does.

State Your Topic and Point of View Clearly

In addition to fulfilling the requirements of the assignment, a strong thesis statement clearly states the specific focus of the essay. Furthermore, it shows your point of view on the topic.

In an informational text, your point of view might be implied, for example by the aspects of the topic that you choose to focus on. In the following example, the author's point of view is implied through a cause-and-effect statement that places blame on the local government:

> *Due to poor communication from the local government, few people in our community are taking part in the town's recycling program.*

In an argument, your point of view, or position, should be stated directly in your thesis statement. Compare the following example with the example above:

> *If the town's local recycling program is to succeed, the local government needs to make better efforts at supporting the program by educating citizens and making recycling bins easier to get.*

Notice how specific these thesis statements are! In particular, notice that the second example not only clearly states the focus of the essay but also previews reasons. It names specific things that the author thinks the local government needs to do: educate citizens and make recycling bins easier to get. One can expect that the rest of the argument will elaborate on these specific ideas.

. . . .

TIP: An assignment or writing prompt might ask you to write an argument to support a claim. Don't let the word *claim* trip you up. Remember (from Lesson 1) that a claim is simply a statement of your point of view or opinion. Essentially, it is the thesis statement for an argument.

. . . .

Engage Your Reader with Your Purpose
Make sure your thesis is interesting, both to you and to your potential readers. If you're not interested in the thesis you are considering, it will show in your writing, and you can be pretty sure your readers won't be interested, either.

A good way to test whether your thesis is interesting and purposeful is to ask the question *So what?* Think about why your topic matters to you and why it should matter to your readers.

For example, compare the following thesis statements:

Local government has failed to communicate necessary information about the town's recycling program.

Due to poor communication from the local government, few people in our community are taking part in the town's recycling program.

Only the second example really explains So what? It clearly illustrates why the failure to communicate information about recycling matters.

A Checklist for Thesis Statement Development

Use the following checklist to help you review and evaluate any thesis statement you write.

A strong thesis statement . . .	A weak thesis statement . . .
is relevant to the assignment.	is off topic.
clearly states the specific focus of the essay.	is vague or general.
reveals your point of view on the topic.	is a simple statement of fact.
reflects a sense of purpose, or why the topic matters to the author and readers.	simply gives information without conveying why it matters.
Sample: Many kids today are watching so much TV that it is affecting their health and ability to learn.	**Sample:** In this essay I will show that kids are watching too much TV.

Should Your Narrative Have a Thesis Statement?

In a **personal narrative**, you tell about an actual experience (rather than an imagined one). In a narrative like this, your job is to reveal, or show, your view of the experience. You might state your point of view directly with a thesis statement, as you would in any other kind of essay. Or you might reveal your point of view indirectly, as you might do in a fictional story.

Whether your personal narrative is in the form of an essay or more like a story, it will be most effective if you reveal your point of view throughout. You do so by showing your reactions to the setting, characters, and events. These reactions not only engage readers but also give them a sense of who you really are and what's important to you.

Practice 1: Revising Thesis Statements

Complete the following chart by providing a strong thesis statement to replace each of the weak thesis statements. Refer to the sample on the chart and the checklist above.

Weak Thesis Statement	Strong Thesis Statement
Video games are very popular.	Video games are stealing time away from homework for many middle school kids in our community.
Sports play a part in school life.	
Kids need more time to goof off.	
Parents nag their kids too much about homework.	

8

Outlining

*I always write a good first line, but I
have trouble in writing the others.*
—MOLIÈRE (1622–1673),
FRENCH PLAYWRIGHT

A well-organized plan can help you write all the sentences that follow your first line. This lesson and the next lesson give you ways to organize your ideas into a plan for writing. It's the conclusion of the planning stage of writing, which is the first step of the writing process outlined in Anchor Standard for Writing 5. Additionally, the organization of ideas, information, and events in your writing is one focus of Standards **W.6.1a, W.6.2a, W.6.3a, W.7.1a, W.7.2a, W.7.3a, W.8.1a, W.8.2a,** and **W.8.3a.**

The most common organizational tool that writers use is the outline, either in rough form or in a more formal and detailed format. An **outline** provides a general sketch or plan for your writing project. Although writing an outline might seem like extra work, the benefits of an outline are numerous.

- An outline provides a path for you to follow once you are immersed in the drafting process.

- An outline can reveal whether your thesis is workable or weak. While outlining, you might find that your thesis is too broad or too narrow or that it does not make an assertion strong enough to support an entire essay.

- An outline can reveal gaps or areas of weakness in the development or support of your central idea or ideas.

- Having an outline can help to relieve any anxiety you might have about writing your composition. There's no need to panic if you have a clear plan!

The Basics of Organization

Whether you are writing an argument, response to literature, informational text, or narrative, your final composition is likely to include an introduction, body, and conclusion. A formal essay, particularly an essay written for school, is likely to be highly structured and include:

- an **introduction**, usually a paragraph long, that introduces the topic and central idea.

- **body paragraphs** that support the central idea.

- a **conclusion**, also usually a paragraph long, that sums things up.

The organization of a narrative is usually based on time rather than on the need to support a central idea. Specifically, a narrative is usually organized in chronological order (which we'll look at in more detail in the next lesson). Therefore, the flow in a narrative from the introduction through the body paragraphs and to the conclusion may be nearly seamless.

Writing an Informal Outline

Whether you're planning an essay or narrative, outlining what goes in the beginning, middle, and end of your composition is likely to be helpful, even if the outline is just a quick, informal summary. Here's an example of an informal outline:

Title: Should Wearing a Uniform Be Required at Our School?

Beginning: a description of tensions/conflicts at our school and quick summary of why a uniform has been suggested
Thesis Statement: An official uniform would be a reasonable way to help relieve tensions among students by creating a more equitable school culture.

Middle
1st body paragraph: reasons why a uniform will be helpful
2nd body paragraph: reactions (quotations, comments) from students and parents in favor
3rd body paragraph: description of the positive outcomes at a similar school
4th body paragraph: a discussion of the possible costs of uniforms
5th body paragraph: reactions (quotations, comments) from students and principal who are against the idea

End
While there has been some serious criticism of the suggested uniform by both students and school leaders, many are in support of the idea. Additionally, there is good evidence that uniforms do create a more democratic atmosphere and reduce tensions among students. An experiment for a year to try out the use of uniforms seems to be an ideal solution to the controversy.

Writing a Formal Outline

A formal outline is more detailed than the previous example. It includes more specific information about the points to be made and the order in which they will be made. Here's an example of a formal outline for the argument on school uniforms:

I. Introduction
   A. Description of tensions/conflicts at our school
   B. Summary of why a uniform has been suggested
   C. Thesis statement: An official uniform should be instituted at our school because it will help to relieve tensions among students and help all students feel equal.
II. Why and how this plan should be adopted
   A. Reasons why a uniform will be helpful
   B. Summary of available statistics on the use of uniforms in the U.S.
   C. Cost analysis of uniforms, with suggestions of how to take care of these costs
III. Local reactions
   A. Summary of and quotations from interview of student leading the protest against uniforms
   B. Quotation from principal, who is against the idea
   C. Summary of and quotations from interview with student body president
   D. Quotations from recent Parents' Association meeting
IV. Case study
   A. Description of how a similar plan was implemented at a similar school
   B. Description of the overwhelmingly positive outcomes there
V. Conclusion and recommendation

TIP: Whether you write an informal outline or a formal one, review it carefully. Does every section you've outlined support or expand upon your thesis statement? If not, then some of the information in your outline might not belong there—or you might need to rethink your thesis.

Practice 1: Writing an Outline

Look again at the brainstorming you did for practice in Lesson 2 and reviewed in Lesson 5. Now write an informal outline for your argument.

If one of the thesis statements you wrote in Lesson 7 appeals to you more, then by all means write an informal outline for an argument based on it. But first, you'll want to brainstorm, freewrite, and/or make an idea web in order to generate some ideas on the topic.

_____

_____

_____

_____

_____

_____

_____

_____

_____

_____

_____

_____

_____

_____

_____

_____

_____

_____

_____

_____

_____

_____

9

Organizational Patterns

Good writing is always a breaking of the soil, clearing away prejudices, pulling up of sour weeds of crooked thinking, stripping the turf so as to get at what is fertile beneath.
—BLAISE CENDRARS (1887–1961),
SWISS NOVELIST AND POET

In this lesson, we'll take a look at some tried and true organizational methods. The organization of ideas, information, and events in your writing is one focus of Standards **W.6.1a, W.6.2a, W.6.3a, W.7.1a, W.7.2a, W.7.3a, W.8.1a, W.8.2a,** and **W.8.3a**.

Your outline shows a plan for organizing the ideas, information, and events you want to write about. But how do you come up with this plan? What method should you use?

Luckily, you don't have to invent your own method. There are several **organizational patterns** to apply in your writing. Each of these patterns helps you emphasize certain relationships among the ideas, events, and details in your composition. Additionally, they help you guide your reader through your essay or narrative, so that he or she is more likely to finish reading with a good understanding of what you hoped to convey.

Let's take a closer look at these patterns, as well as some ways to apply them.

Sequential or Chronological Order

This organizational pattern involves telling about events in the order in which they occur (or occurred). This pattern can be used in narratives and when describing processes.

For example, an outline for an account of the early history of your town might follow this pattern:

    I. 1600s
        A. Native settlements
        B. First English settlements

    II. early 1700s, up to the French and Indian War
        A. The economy
        B. Daily life

    III. late 1700s
        A. French and Indian War
        B. American Revolution
        C. After the American Revolution

An outline for the description of a process might be as simple as the following:

    I. Step 1
    II. Step 2
    III. Step 3
    IV. Step 4

Order of Importance or Emphasis

This organizational pattern involves giving information in order of its importance or emphasis. For example, an outline for an argument might follow this general pattern:

    I. Important reason to support the claim
       A. Supporting information/detail #1
       B. Supporting information/detail #2
       C. Supporting information/detail #3

    II. An even more important reason to support the claim
       A. Supporting information/detail #1
       B. Supporting information/detail #2
       C. Supporting information/detail #3

    III. The most important reason to support the claim
       A. Supporting information/detail #1
       B. Supporting information/detail #2
       C. Supporting information/detail #3

Similarly, information can be organized from general (or simplest) to specific (or more complex) or vice versa. For example, you can start an essay with an overview of the topic or background information before diving into the specifics that you really want your reader to understand. Or you can start with a specific anecdote or example of a trend before revealing the bigger picture.

A definition can be organized from general to specific. In a **definition**, you explain the meaning or significance of a word, phrase, or concept. Here, for example, is an outline for an essay defining what makes a good citizen:

    I. What is a good citizen?
       A. Definition of *citizen*

    II. Qualities of a good citizen
       A. Takes care of the community
       B. Participates by voting, speaking to representatives, etc.
       C. Fights for what's fair

III. Examples of good citizens
    A. Example of an extraordinary good citizen: Rosa Parks
    B. Example of an ordinary good citizen: my mom

The definition starts generally, by defining the word *citizen*, before it describes the qualities of a good citizen. It concludes with specifics, by giving examples of good citizens, both extraordinary and ordinary.

Compare and Contrast

Writing an essay in which you **compare** (tell about similarities) and **contrast** (tell about differences) two subjects is one way to shine new light on one or both of your subjects. However, keep in mind that such an essay is unlikely to be interesting or informative unless you are comparing things that share significant points of comparison. For example, it wouldn't make sense to compare and contrast completely unlike things, such as jumping rope with having a cat as a pet. But you could easily compare and contrast having a cat as a pet with having a dog as a pet.

There are two ways to organize a compare-and-contrast essay. One way is to compare and contrast specific aspects of the two things you are comparing and contrasting, point by point. Here's an example of this approach for an essay comparing and contrasting cats and dogs as pets:

I. Temperament and behavior
    A. The temperament and behavior of cats
    B. The temperament and behavior of dogs

II. Care
    A. Caring for cats
    B. Caring for dogs

The other way is to discuss similarities together and differences together.

I. Similarities between cats and dogs
    A. Similarities in temperament and behavior
    B. Similarities in care

II. Differences between cats and dogs
    A. Differences in temperament and behavior
    B. Differences in care

Cause and Effect

Writing essays about causes, effects, and both causes and effects is another way to shine light on a subject. Just as with compare-and-contrast essays, there are two ways to organize a cause-and-effect essay. One way is to tell about causes and immediate effects point by point. Here's an example of this approach for an essay about the causes of the Great Depression:

    I. Cause: 1929 stock market crash
       A. Lost confidence in banks
       B. People buying fewer things

    II. Cause: Bank failures
       A. Lost savings
       B. People buying fewer things
       C. Less production and lost jobs

    III. Cause: Drought
       A. Less farm production and lost jobs
       B. Migration

The other way is to tell about causes together and effects together. For example:

    I. Causes of the Great Depression
       A. 1929 stock market crash
       B. Bank failures
       C. Drought

    II. Effects of these causes
       A. People buying fewer things
       B. Less production and lost jobs
       C. Migration

Problem and Solution

The purpose of an argument is often to propose a solution to a problem. A common way to organize such an argument is first to tell about the problem and then to tell about the proposed solution. Here's an example of this approach:

    I. Problem: School lunches are unhealthy and unappealing.
       A. Too much processed food is offered.
       B. Not enough fruits and vegetables are offered.

    II. Solution: Start a school garden and salad bar.
       A. A garden means more fruits and vegetables for school lunches.
       B. Growing good food gets kids interested in good food.
       C. Salad bars also make fruits and veggies appealing.

A similar organizational pattern could be used to tell about the advantages (pros) and disadvantages (cons) related to a topic or proposal. The informal outline in Lesson 8 gives one example of this organizational pattern. Here's another example of this approach, for an essay weighing the pros and cons of the school-garden proposal:

    I. School garden cons
       A. Too costly?
       B. Too much work?

    II. School garden pros
       A. More fruits and vegetables for school lunches
       B. Kids more interested in good food by growing it

A strong argument is likely to incorporate a discussion of counterclaims. In other words, rather than ignoring any reasonable objections or disadvantages of a proposed solution, it addresses those possible cons directly, as in the following example.

    I. Problem: School lunches are unhealthy and unappealing.
       A. Too much processed food is offered.
       B. Not enough fruits and vegetables are offered.

II. Solution: Start a school garden and salad bar.
   A. A garden means more fruits and vegetables for school lunches.
   B. Salad bars also make fruits and veggies appealing.

III. School garden cons
   A. Too costly?
   B. Too much work?

IV. Responses to school garden cons
   A. Costs could be paid for by cutting back on purchases of other (unhealthy) foods.
   B. The work is worthwhile, because growing good food gets kids interested in good food.

Spatial Order

This organizational pattern is usually used for physical descriptions of objects or places. It involves describing something from its top to bottom, outside to inside, left to right, or near to far, and so on. For example, you might describe the outside of a building and then its interior. Or you might describe a landscape by telling first about the mountains in the distance, then about a nearby lake, and finally about the little cottage on the shore of the lake, where your characters live. This organizational pattern helps your readers visualize the objects and places you are describing as though they are experiencing them directly.

An outline for an informational text on the geography of your state might follow this pattern, organizing information by location:

I. The coast
   1. Landforms and climate
   2. Economy
   3. Major towns and cities

II. The western region
   1. Landforms and climate
   2. Economy
   3. Major towns and cities

III. The central region
   1. Landforms and climate
   2. Economy
   3. Major towns and cities

IV. The eastern region
   1. Landforms and climate
   2. Economy
   3. Major towns and cities

Classification by Subtopic or Type

This organizational pattern is the most flexible and can almost always be used when no other pattern works. In this pattern, you break down the broader topic into subtopics, and you name, or **classify**, each subtopic according to its type. For example, the description of a nation would involve descriptions of its geology, government, economy, culture, and history.

The formal outline in Lesson 8 is an example of this organizational pattern. The subtopics are overview, local response, and case study.

. . . .

TIP: Sometimes you might combine several organizational patterns in one essay. For example, let's say you are writing an essay on butterflies. You might begin by describing the physical characteristics of a butterfly (spatial order), go on to describe the life cycle of a butterfly (sequential order), and conclude by comparing and contrasting butterflies and moths (compare and contrast).

. . . .

Practice 1: Reorganizing an Outline

Look back at the example outlines given in Lesson 8. Remember, the organizational pattern of the informal outline is pro and con, and the organizational pattern of the formal outline is classification by subtopic. Write another outline for the argument on school uniforms with a problem-and-solution organizational pattern.

Practice 2: Selecting Another Organizational Pattern

Look back at the outline you wrote for practice in Lesson 8. What organizational pattern does it follow? Select a different organizational pattern for your argument, and write another outline based on that pattern.

_____

_____

_____

_____

_____

_____

_____

_____

_____

_____

_____

_____

_____

_____

_____

_____

_____

_____

_____

_____

_____

10

Planning for On-Demand Writing

I write rhymes with addition and algebra, mental geometry.
—Ice-T (1958–),
American rapper and actor

This lesson gives you a plan for those times when you're asked to produce a piece of writing in a short amount of time. Anchor Standard for Writing 10 requires students to practice writing in both extended and brief time frames, including a single sitting.

Throughout your time in school, you will be asked to complete **on-demand writing tasks**. These tasks—usually tests—require you to write an essay (or, in some cases, a narrative) in response to a prompt and within a limited time frame.

- In-class exams in any of your courses might include one or more essay questions.

- One or more of your state standardized tests might include short-answer or essay questions.

■ High school and college entrance exams such as the SAT might include an essay-writing component.

Even though the time you have to write a composition in any of these situations is limited—and may be brief—taking some of that time to plan your writing is essential. The four steps in planning for on-demand writing include the following:

1. Organizing your time
2. Understanding the prompt
3. Reading or viewing any materials
4. Organizing your ideas

Organizing Your Time

Although taking *some* time to plan your writing is essential, it's also essential that you don't take up *all* of your time with planning. Otherwise, you could find yourself without a finished composition when the test proctor tells you that time's up!

Let's say that you have 45 minutes to write an essay for an in-class exam, and there are no materials to read or review. You might decide to take 10 minutes to read and understand the prompt and organize your ideas, which would leave you with 35 minutes to write and review your essay. If the exam starts at 11:10, then you know that you should start writing by 11:20. Write "writing by 11:20" at the top of the page you'll be using for your outline, and be sure to check the clock on occasion.

Or let's say that you have one hour to write an essay in response to two readings. In this case, you might give yourself 15 minutes to understand the prompt and study the readings, 10 minutes to organize your ideas, and 35 minutes to write and review your essay. Again, note the times when you should transition from activity to activity at the top of the page you'll be using to take notes or for your outline.

As you can see, this step in planning for on-demand writing involves making just one or two quick decisions. Don't spend more than a few seconds on this step!

. . . .

TIP: Information about the structure and timing of standardized tests is typically available to the public. Find out what's involved in taking the test *before* test day. If there are one or more essays on the test, you can show up for the test already with a plan in place for organizing your writing time.

. . . .

Understanding the Prompt

Understanding the prompt is the most crucial part of an on-demand writing task. Even if you write a beautiful composition, if it doesn't fulfill the requirements of the prompt, it won't be scored well.

Some prompts, such as the following, are brief and don't offer much information.

> *Write about a time when you made a new friend.*

Other prompts, such as the following, are lengthy and specify exactly what is expected.

> *Good friendships may begin unexpectedly, based on chance. Some good friends start off by disliking each other. And other times, good friends become close almost immediately.*
>
> *Write a narrative telling about a time when you made a new friend. Your narrative may tell about meeting a friend for the first time. Or your narrative may tell about the moment when you and someone you already knew first became friends. In your narrative, show what you think makes a good friend.*
>
> *Be sure that your narrative:*
>
> - *is based on a specific point of view.*
> - *reveals one or more characters.*
> - *uses vivid and exact language to bring characters and events to life.*
> - *has an effective conclusion.*

Given either type of prompt, your task in understanding the prompt is to decide the following:

- What topic should you write about or question should you answer?

- For what purpose should you write—for example, to argue, inform, or tell a story?

- What kinds of evidence or details should you include?

- What audience does the prompt suggest, and what role should you assume, if any? For example, a prompt might tell you to imagine that you are an applicant for a job.

Practice 1: Understanding a Prompt

Review the longer sample prompt above. Underline the sentence that identifies the topic and text type that are required. Then underline the sentence that identifies what the evidence and details in your writing should show.

Reading or Viewing Materials

Some prompts may be accompanied by materials for reading or viewing. These may include pieces of literature, photographs, advertisements, political cartoons, graphs, and other documents you are asked to analyze. Or these may include articles and/or graphic material that include information you can use to support your thesis or claim.

No matter what materials you are given to read or view, read them and examine them with a purpose.

- Check the clock, and be sure to stick to the amount of time you initially allotted for reading and viewing.

- Set your purpose. Why are you reading? What are you looking for? Are you analyzing a poem in terms of a question given in the prompt? Or are you seeking facts, examples, and quotations to use as evidence? Keep this purpose in mind as you read and examine the materials.

■ Read and view actively. Underline parts of readings that you want to refer to in your writing. Jot down notes in the margin.

Organizing Your Ideas

Once you've considered the prompt and any reading or viewing materials, take the time to do a bit of outlining, even just a rough outline. If you are really, truly pressed for time, at least take a few moments to write down the following:

■ Your thesis statement, which you should keep in mind at all times during the writing process. Make sure that every sentence you write supports your thesis. After all, you don't have time to lose focus!

■ The two or three main ideas you plan to cover in your essay.

■ The conclusion you want to draw, which should be more than a simple restatement of your thesis. It should represent an expansion of your thesis that develops out of the support you give your thesis.

. . . .

TIP: If you have the space to do so, write on every other line of the page. This way, you'll have a bit of room for any minor corrections you might want to make when you check your composition.

Indeed, giving yourself time to check your writing is as important as giving yourself time to plan it. First, review the prompt again, and check that you have responded to its requirements thoroughly and appropriately. Next, read your writing to improve any vague or sloppy language or correct errors in language use, spelling, or punctuation. If you decide to insert a lengthier passage, write it on a clean page (or part of the page) and use an asterisk to guide your reader from where the passage should be inserted to where it is written.

. . . .

Practice 2: Outlining an On-Demand Narrative

Review the longer sample prompt given in this lesson. Using the guidelines given above, write a rough outline for a response to this prompt.

_____

_____

_____

_____

_____

_____

_____

_____

_____

_____

_____

_____

_____

_____

_____

_____

_____

_____

_____

_____

_____

_____

_____

Section 3

Writing Your First Draft

At last, it's time to start writing! But even as you write your first draft, your goal isn't perfection. Forget about perfection! Your only goal is to get a draft down, from beginning to end. In this section, we'll go over both the process of drafting and the elements of a complete draft. Let's get started!

11

Beginning Your Draft

Very few writers know what they are doing until they've done it.
—ANNE LAMOTT (1954–   ),
AMERICAN NOVELIST AND NONFICTION WRITER

In this lesson, we'll go over the drafting process and then take a look at some strategies for writing attention-getting beginnings. Introducing your claim, topic, or point of view and engaging readers are among the focuses of Standards **W.6.1a, W.6.2a, W.6.3a, W.7.1a, W.7.2a, W.7.3a, W.8.1a, W.8.2a,** and **W.8.3a.**

To *draft* is to write provisional, or temporary, versions of what will become your finished piece of writing. Whether you are writing an urgent, serious argument or a comical narrative, your aim should be to draft and revise—possibly a few (or many) times. It is a rare writer who can produce a well-polished piece of writing in just one draft.

The purpose of your first draft—often called the **rough draft**—is to get your ideas down on paper so that you can go back and revise, expand, and polish them up into a finished composition.

Writing the Rough Draft

Think of the rough draft as a sketch drawn from the plan you developed during the prewriting stage. This draft includes everything you want to say (or think you want to say) from beginning to end. However, the details are likely not yet all filled in, and the language is likely not yet quite right.

Here are some tips for writing this first draft:

- Although you'll want your rough draft to have a beginning, middle, and end, you don't actually have to write it from beginning to end. For example, some writers prefer to write the body paragraphs before working on the introduction.

- As you write, you should keep your purpose and audience in mind and aim for an appropriate tone, but you still don't need to worry too much about writing very well (as long as you give yourself plenty of time—see below). Do try to write in sentences and paragraphs, however.

- Start writing your rough draft early enough so that you have time to revise and polish it.

- Remember the accordion analogy introduced in Lesson 5. Your composition may expand and contract several times from version to version. So don't worry too much about the length of your rough draft. If you write out your ideas in sentences and paragraphs from beginning to end, you'll see whether you need to develop your ideas further or focus them.

But what if you find that you're completely blocked—and unable to write a single sentence? There are several ways to break through.

- Try freewriting on your topic. You could freewrite about all your complaints about your topic or the assignment. Or you could try freewriting your rough draft. Set out your outline so you can follow it as you write—and go!

- Talk to a parent, a friend, or another trusted person about what you are hoping to say.

- Read a published article or story in a form similar to the form you are writing, to absorb its structure, strategies, and use of language.

- Go back and reread the assignment; you may be missing a big clue.

- Give it a rest, overnight if possible, and then come back to your work with fresh eyes the next day.

• •

TIP: The best writers, of course, don't just read to get help when they're blocked. They read all the time. In fact, one of the most effective ways to improve your writing doesn't involve writing at all. If you read regularly, your writing will almost certainly improve.

• •

Hooking the Reader

Although, as we said above, you don't actually have to start your rough draft at the beginning, in the rest of this lesson, we're going to focus on beginnings. Specifically, we're going to focus on the very first sentence or sentences of your composition. These are the sentences that grab your reader's attention and engage him or her with your topic and point of view.

Here are seven techniques for grabbing your reader's attention:

1. Begin with a shocking statement that engages readers and gets them thinking about your topic right away. Remember (from Lesson 2) the student who, after brainstorming about global warming, decided to write about its effects on polar bears? She could open her essay with a shock like this:

   In 50 years, there will be no more polar bears on the planet.

   Notice the authority of this statement. The sentence doesn't say, "In 50 years, there may be no more polar bears on the planet" or "There's a possibility that in 50 years, there will be no more polar bears on the planet." Much of the shock in the statement is in the boldness of the claim.

2. You can also get readers thinking about your topic by asking an engaging question about it.

    Are you willing to watch a polar bear die of starvation?

    Notice that this question challenges the reader with the suggestion that there may actually be starving polar bears. Compare this opening question with one that asks, simply, "Is global warming harming polar bears?" This question is an acceptable opening to an essay, but it doesn't demand that readers care in the way that the previous example does.

3. Begin with a compelling quotation, particularly from an authority on your subject.

    "In a shrinking ice environment, the ability of polar bears to find food, to reproduce, and to survive will all be reduced," said Scott Schliebe, the leader of the Alaskan polar bear project for the U.S. Fish and Wildlife Service, in 2005. "Polar bears don't have a place to go if they lose the ice."

    Finding a quotation strong enough to serve as your opening statement can be difficult, but it may be worth the hunt. If you haven't found a good quotation in print (and if you have the time), you might consider interviewing someone with expertise or experience related to your topic. They just might say something worth quoting!

4. Describe an imaginary scenario.

    Imagine a world with no ice pack left in the Arctic Circle—and no more polar bears.

    Be sure that the scenario you propose is believable. You want to engage your reader—not give him or her a reason to dismiss your thinking as too far out.

5. Describe an actual character or scene.

    The polar regions are home to ice, wind, and temperatures far below freezing. Winter nights can go on and on for months. And yet what looks to most of us like an inhospitable wasteland is home to many kinds of wildlife, including polar bears.

A vivid description can reveal a character or set the scene in a way that brings your subject to life for your readers. It's a particularly effective way to begin a narrative.

. . . .

TIP: You can even begin a narrative in medias res. This Latin term means "in the middle of things." Instead of slowly introducing characters or the setting, just drop the reader into the middle of an unfolding event or dialogue. If the scene you've created is compelling, the reader will be immediately engaged.

. . . .

6. Offer one or more examples or share an **anecdote**, or brief story, that illustrates your thesis.

   The news on polar bears these days isn't good. Research scientists in the Canadian Wildlife Service are reporting dramatic declines in the polar bear population. Additionally, eyewitness accounts by field workers describe the bears as growing visibly skinnier because they can't find enough food.

   The specific examples presented in this opening—a declining population, visibly skinny bears—make the crisis for polar bears seem urgently real. An anecdote can have a similar effect. For instance:

   Global warming may be a difficult subject for the individual to grasp, but field workers in the Canadian Wildlife Service are seeing this global problem in very local terms as they conduct their annual count of polar bears on the western coast of Manitoba.

   Notice how quickly this opening brings the subject from the general (global warming) to the particular (the Canadian Wildlife Service's annual count of polar bears in a certain region of Manitoba).

7. Finally, you could adapt a familiar quotation for your own purposes.

   To be concerned about global warming, or not: That is the question facing every person in the world right now.

This allusion to Hamlet's famous speech about his moral dilemma highlights the seriousness of the topic. It also catches the reader's attention with its wit.

Practice 1: Evaluating Openings

The following chart presents pairs of introductory sentences. Circle the stronger sentence in each pair. Then write a brief explanation of why the sentence you chose is more likely to grab the reader's attention.

Introductory sentences	How does your choice grab the reader's attention?
1. I've lived in this town my whole life and never knew there was an underground tunnel. 2. I've lived in this town my whole life and never knew its best-kept secret.	
1. Baseball is an extremely boring game. 2. Baseball is so boring it could put the dead to sleep.	
1. The Internet is turning us all into zombies. 2. The controversy surrounding the effects of the Internet on its users continues to be a hot topic among research scientists.	
1. My favorite movie is Star Wars, for a reason you would not suspect. 2. Star Wars is probably one of the five best movies ever made.	

12

Writing the Introduction

The worst thing you can do is censor yourself as the pencil hits the paper. You must not edit until you get it all on paper.
—STEPHEN SONDHEIM (1930–),
AMERICAN COMPOSER AND LYRICIST

Your introduction needs to do more than grab the reader's attention. In this lesson, we'll go over all of the elements of a good introduction. Introducing your claim, topic, or point of view and engaging readers are among the focuses of Standards **W.6.1a**, **W.6.2a**, **W.6.3a**, **W.7.1a**, **W.7.2a**, **W.7.3a**, **W.8.1a**, **W.8.2a**, and **W.8.3a**.

As you saw in Lesson 8, essays typically have three parts: an introduction, a body, and a conclusion. An introduction may comprise one or two paragraphs (or more, if your composition is especially long). Its main purpose is to give readers a good idea of what the overall composition is about, in a way that entices them to keep reading.

The Structure of a Good Introduction

In an essay, a good introduction includes four elements.

1. First, it grabs the reader's attention.
2. Next, it provides necessary background information on your topic.
3. Finally, it states your thesis clearly and concisely.
4. Throughout, it establishes a tone for the overall composition.

Let's look at each of these four elements in the introduction to an essay on the classic film *King Kong*.

Grabbing the Reader's Attention

Based on what you learned from the examples in the previous chapter, which do you think is the better opening?

> *I'm going to write about my favorite movie, which is* King Kong.

> King Kong *is one of the saddest monsters in movie history.*

The second example, of course, is the better one. The first example gives the reader no compelling reason to continue reading. Why should the reader care what the writer's favorite movie is? In contrast, the second example gives the reader a good reason to be interested and continue reading to find out why this statement may be true.

Providing Background Information

The reason for including background information in your introduction should be to give the reader some context for understanding your thesis statement. Consider the following excerpts from two introductory paragraphs:

> *King Kong is one of the saddest monsters in movie history. He lived on an island called Skull Island. He got sent to New York and was exhibited as a monster for people to stare at. He falls in love with a girl named Ann, and eventually, he is killed on the Empire State Building.*

> *King Kong is one of the saddest monsters in movie history. When we first see him in the 1933 film titled* King Kong, *the giant gorilla is living*

among dinosaurs in a remote and sinister place called Skull Island. Kong seems to be the only gorilla there, so his life is clearly a lonely one. And things don't get any better for him when he is captured and taken to New York City to be exhibited as the Eighth Wonder of the World.

Again, the second example is the better one. It identifies the movie that is the subject of the essay, "the 1933 film titled *King Kong*." It indicates that King Kong is a "giant gorilla." And it builds on the idea that King Kong is "one of the saddest monsters" by mentioning his lonely life in "a remote and sinister place."

Stating the Thesis

Now read the complete introduction to the essay on *King Kong*.

> *King Kong is one of the saddest monsters in movie history. When we first see him in the 1933 film titled* King Kong, *the giant gorilla is living among dinosaurs in a remote and sinister place called Skull Island. Kong seems to be the only gorilla there, so his life is clearly a lonely one. And things don't get any better for him when he is captured and taken to New York City to be exhibited as the Eighth Wonder of the World. Even though Kong causes terror and destruction there, it is his desperation that makes* King Kong *such a compelling and influential film.*

Do you see how the background information builds on the opening sentence in a way that leads right to the thesis statement?

Remember the elements of a strong thesis statement from Lesson 7.

- It fulfills the requirements of the assignment (if there is an assignment).

- It clearly states the topic and your point of view.

- It engages readers with your purpose by answering the question *So what?*

How does a thesis statement answer the question So what? Compare the following thesis statements:

> *Even though Kong causes terror and destruction in New York City, he does it because he is desperate.*

Even though Kong causes terror and destruction in New York City, it is his desperation that makes King Kong *such a compelling and influential film.*

Only the second example shows why King Kong's desperation matters.

Establishing the Tone

How would you describe the tone of the introduction to the essay on *King Kong*? It's pretty formal, right? By using this formal tone, the author is showing us, his audience, that he wants us to take his ideas about an old monster movie seriously.

Remember the close relationship between your purpose for writing, your audience, and your tone. Match your tone with your purpose carefully.

. . . .

TIP: If you're having trouble drafting an introduction, remember that you can always skip it and write your body paragraphs first. After you have a sense of how your ideas are developing, you can go back to the beginning and draft a first paragraph.

. . . .

Introducing a Narrative

All four elements of a good introduction to an essay may not apply if you're writing a narrative. In particular, your narrative might not have a thesis statement. Nevertheless, you still want to grab your reader's attention, provide context for understanding your story, and establish the tone.

See, for example, the opening paragraph of Joshua Slocum's 1900 memoir titled *Sailing Alone Around the World.*

> *In the fair land of Nova Scotia, a maritime province, there is a ridge called North Mountain, overlooking the Bay of Fundy on one side and the fertile Annapolis valley on the other. On the northern slope of the range grows the hardy spruce-tree, well adapted for ship-timbers, of which many vessels of all classes have been built. The people of this coast, hardy, robust, and strong, are disposed to compete in the world's commerce, and*

it is nothing against the master mariner if the birthplace mentioned on his certificate be Nova Scotia. I was born in a cold spot, on coldest North Mountain, on a cold February 20, though I am a citizen of the United States—a naturalized Yankee, if it may be said that Nova Scotians are not Yankees in the truest sense of the word. On both sides my family were sailors; and if any Slocum should be found not seafaring, he will show at least an inclination to whittle models of boats and contemplate voyages. My father was the sort of man who, if wrecked on a desolate island, would find his way home, if he had a jack-knife and could find a tree. He was a good judge of a boat, but the old clay farm which some calamity made his was an anchor to him. He was not afraid of a capful of wind, and he never took a back seat at a camp-meeting or a good, old-fashioned revival.

As for myself, the wonderful sea charmed me from the first. . . .

This paragraph offers basic information about Slocum's life, such as where and when he was born. But its main purpose is not to give these facts but to introduce a world where people are "hardy, robust, and strong" and love sailing. The focus is entirely on the setting and characters, which are described in a way that is captivating even as it introduces central themes (sailing, self-sufficiency). For example, just look at Slocum's description of his father: "My father was the sort of man who, if wrecked on a desolate island, would find his way home, if he had a jack-knife and could find a tree." It's no wonder that Slocum himself grew up to be the first person to sail around the world by himself!

Practice 1: Drafting an Introduction

In Lesson 7 you wrote thesis statements for practice, and in Lessons 8 and 9 you wrote outlines for practice. Choose one of these and draft an introductory paragraph for an argument based on the thesis or outline you chose. Include all four elements of a good introduction to an essay: an opening that grabs the reader's attention, necessary background information, a clearly stated thesis, and an appropriate tone.

_____

_____

_____

_____

_____

_____

_____

_____

_____

_____

_____

_____

_____

_____

_____

_____

_____

_____

13

Writing the Body Paragraphs

A scrupulous writer, in every sentence that he writes, will ask himself at least four questions, thus: 1. What am I trying to say? 2. What words will express it? 3. What image or idiom will make it clearer? 4. Is this image fresh enough to have an effect?
—George Orwell (1903–1950),
British novelist and essayist

This lesson gives an overview of the structure of a good supporting paragraph and describes specific ways to support the thesis of an essay. These elements of writing are among those discussed in Standards **W.6.1b**, **W.6.2b**, **W.6.9**, **W.7.1b**, **W.7.2b**, **W.7.9**, **W.8.1b**, **W.8.2b**, and **W.8.9**.

The same care you put into writing your first paragraph should be given to all subsequent paragraphs. Their role is to support and develop the ideas and themes with which you engaged your reader at the start. Additionally, you want your body paragraphs to keep your reader engaged by providing lively and compelling reasons to keep reading.

Requirements of a Good Paragraph

Paragraphs are, of course, the building blocks of all written work. Paragraphs aren't formed by arbitrary breaks in your writing; they are created to serve specific purposes.

- They group ideas in a way that helps readers understand them.

- They indicate shifts in subject matter, time, or (in the case of printed dialogue) speaker.

- They give readers' eyes a bit of rest.

· ·

TIP: The length of your paragraphs matters. Extremely long paragraphs, for example, may be difficult to read. They might also indicate that the relationships between the ideas or events in your composition have not really been worked out. A series of very short paragraphs, on the other hand, may seem choppy or disconnected. They might also indicate that a thesis is not well developed. However, when used carefully, one-sentence paragraphs can make a dramatic impact, although not if overdone.

· ·

In an essay, a well-developed body paragraph usually follows a general pattern.

- It begins with a **transition** from the previous paragraph. This transition might be a word (such as *furthermore*), a phrase (such as *in addition*), or an entire sentence. Its purpose is to connect the ideas in the previous paragraph with the ideas in the paragraph it begins. (See Lessons 14 and 18 for more on transitions.)

- It includes a topic sentence that presents the main idea of the paragraph. This main idea should focus on one aspect of the thesis statement.

- It explains the main idea further, if necessary.

- It provides one or more examples that support the main idea. These examples could be facts, definitions, details, quotations, or anecdotes.

- It explains the examples.

- It concludes by wrapping up the paragraph and transitioning to the next paragraph.

An effective paragraph, therefore, does much more than just list facts and examples. It includes explanations that make connections between your ideas, facts, and examples. In order to make these connections, ask the following kinds of questions:

- How does this fact or example relate to the thesis? How does it relate to the other facts or examples I found?

- Why is this fact or example interesting? Why is it important?

- What does this fact or example imply?

By asking these questions, you may discover that some of the facts or details that you were planning to write about do not actually belong in your essay. Even if it's interesting, if a fact doesn't relate to your thesis statement, don't include it.

Support for Your Thesis

So what kind of information *should* you include in your body paragraphs? Remember the chart in Lesson 5, which lists the different kinds of supporting ideas, information, and details you may include in different types of texts. Here's more information on each of these kinds of support:

1. Provide logical and compelling reasons.

In any essay, particularly an argument, that reflects a strong and particular point of view, give your reader logical and compelling reasons to understand and agree with you. Here are some reasons the writer of the essay on *King Kong* could provide to support his thesis (*Even though Kong causes terror and destruction, it is his desperation that makes* King Kong *such a compelling and influential film*):

> **Weak reason:** *"I couldn't stop crying at the end of the movie; it was just totally sad."* (This reason is too subjective.)

Better reason: *"One has only to mention the name* 'King Kong' *and moviegoers' eyes will tear up. He has become the very symbol of brutalized innocence."* (Instead of appealing to readers with his own emotional reaction to the film, here the writer describes the response of "moviegoers." This could be a good reason to accept the idea that King Kong's desperation is widely compelling—but do moviegoers actually tear up at the sound of his name?)

Best reason: *"The multiple remakes of this movie reveal the profound emotional impact that* King Kong *has had on fans and filmmakers alike."* (Now, here's a fact-based reason that the writer can really build on!)

. . . .

TIP: It is wise to consider all the reasons a reader might *not* agree with you. Don't ignore or dismiss opposing views. Take them up, address them, and give your reason or reasons for seeing otherwise.

. . . .

2. Provide specific examples and concrete and sensory details.

In all text types, specific examples and concrete details make your ideas vivid and real for the reader. Remember these sentences from the paragraph on *King Kong*, which describes Kong as "living among dinosaurs in a remote and sinister place called Skull Island" where he "seems to be the only gorilla." Such details make Kong's isolation seem vivid and real. The reader can picture why the writer says that Kong is "the saddest monster in movie history."

Adding more sensory details—that is, details about sight, sound, smell, taste, and touch—would also be helpful. For example, in writing in a body paragraph about Kong's terror in captivity, the writer might mention Kong's bellowing. Imagining the sound of Kong's fear would help the reader understand his sorrow.

3. Provide facts and definitions.

Facts are things that are known (or at least generally agreed) to be true. And definitions explain the meaning or significance of a word, phrase, or concept. Put more plainly, facts and definitions are ways of discussing reality in an objective manner. Therefore, they may form the very essence of an informational text. They are also a great way to support your claim in an argument.

To support the argument about the importance of *King Kong* in movie history, for example, the writer might provide facts about the movie's influence on the history of film. How many times has the movie been adapted or remade? How many other movie monsters have been patterned after Kong? Remember, however, to include only facts that are clearly relevant to your thesis. For example, the Kong writer might include facts about the length of the film or the subsequent career of its leading actress, Fay Wray, but none of these facts is likely to support the thesis. A good rule to follow is: Make it relevant, or leave it out.

4. Include anecdotes and descriptions.

At times it may even be appropriate to include a personal anecdote that supports your thesis. For example, if you are writing about a controversial topic, such as whether or not your school should adopt an official uniform, an anecdote about your experience at a school that required uniforms might be illuminating. However, such anecdotes provide good support only when they relate directly to the topic and illustrate a particular point about the topic.

Similarly, descriptions of specific events or situations that pertain to your topic may be informative. For example, an essay on school uniforms could include descriptions of the uniforms themselves and descriptions of schools that have adopted uniforms.

5. Include quotations.

Quotations are a great way to incorporate other voices and views on your subject into an essay. They are a particularly effective way to support your claim in an argument, because they show that others share your perspectives. Additionally, quotations from people who have special insight or expertise in your subject lend authority to your views. For example, a quotation from a film critic who has written an entire book about King Kong might give some heft to our Kong writer's argument, as in the following example:

> *In* Tracking King Kong: A Hollywood Icon in World Culture, *Cynthia Marie Erb suggests that "like James Bond, Scarlett O'Hara, Batman, and the* Star Trek *characters, King Kong has become a cultural*

phenomenon—a character repeatedly featured in advertisements, political cartoons, musicals, operas, novels, comic books, film sequels, music videos, and other cultural works" (14).

· ·

TIP: If you're writing a response to literature, including quotations from the work or works of literature you're writing about isn't only recommended—it's just about required. After all, what better way is there to provide examples that support your interpretation?

· ·

6. Include graphics.

Finally, graphic features, such as those described below, can help you support or develop the ideas you present in your essay.

- **Photographs or illustrations** can be used to show what a person, place, or event looked like.

- **Maps** can be used to provide additional information about a place you are writing about.

- **Charts or graphs** can be used to present statistics or the results of a survey or experiment in an orderly way.

- **Tables** can be used to summarize or compare information.

- **Diagrams** can be used to show processes or the parts of things.

- **Timelines** can be used to outline sequences of events.

· ·

TIP: In an argument, the information, examples, and quotations given to support your claim are often called the **evidence**. The best evidence is evidence that your audience will find convincing. Remember this idea as you think about what evidence to include. For example, think about whether your audience will be most convinced by a personal anecdote or by data from a survey. And think about what kinds of quotations your audience will find most convincing.

· ·

Practice 1: Supporting a Thesis

You've read one writer's introduction to an essay about a favorite movie, and you've seen some ideas about how he could support his thesis. Now identify your favorite movie, draft a thesis statement for an essay about it, and write down three kinds of support you could include in the essay, with examples.

My Favorite Movie:	
My Proposed Thesis Statement:	
Three Kinds of Support:	
1.	
2.	
3.	

14

Writing the Body of a Narrative

True ease in writing comes from art, not chance,
As those move easiest who have learn'd to dance.
—ALEXANDER POPE (1688–1744),
BRITISH POET

This lesson explains ways to bring a scene to life in a narrative, as discussed in Standards **W.6.3b**, **W.7.3b**, and **W.8.3b**.

Remember that the organization of a narrative is typically based on time (usually chronological order) rather than on the need to support a central idea. Instead of providing information and evidence, the body of a narrative develops the story, telling about experiences and revealing their meaning.

Narrative Techniques

First, let's look at another excerpt from Joshua Slocum's memoir. This excerpt describes the beginning of his journey across the Atlantic Ocean.

On the evening of July 5 the Spray, after having steered all day over a lumpy sea, took it into her head to go without the helmsman's aid. I had been steering southeast by south, but the wind hauling forward a bit, she dropped into a smooth lane, heading southeast, and making about eight knots, her very best work. I crowded on sail to cross the track of the liners without loss of time, and to reach as soon as possible the friendly Gulf Stream. The fog lifting before night, I was afforded a look at the sun just as it was touching the sea. I watched it go down and out of sight. Then I turned my face eastward, and there, apparently at the very end of the bowsprit, was the smiling full moon rising out of the sea. Neptune himself coming over the bows could not have startled me more. "Good evening, sir," I cried; "I'm glad to see you." Many a long talk since then I have had with the man in the moon; he had my confidence on the voyage.

About midnight the fog shut down again denser than ever before. One could almost "stand on it." It continued so for a number of days, the wind increasing to a gale. The waves rose high, but I had a good ship. Still, in the dismal fog I felt myself drifting into loneliness, an insect on a straw in the midst of the elements. I lashed the helm, and my vessel held her course, and while she sailed I slept.

During these days a feeling of awe crept over me. My memory worked with startling power. The ominous, the insignificant, the great, the small, the wonderful, the commonplace—all appeared before my mental vision in magical succession. Pages of my history were recalled which had been so long forgotten that they seemed to belong to a previous existence. I heard all the voices of the past laughing, crying, telling what I had heard them tell in many corners of the earth.

The loneliness of my state wore off when the gale was high and I found much work to do. When fine weather returned, then came the sense of solitude, which I could not shake off. . . .

Notice the variety of narrative techniques used in this excerpt. A **narrative technique** is a method used to tell a story, such as description and dialogue. Narrative techniques help to dramatize a scene instead of just telling what happened. Here, they bring the experience of sailing to life for the reader, and they also reveal Slocum's character.

Transitions and Language About Time

Transitions and words and phrases that indicate time not only keep the sequence of events clear but also keep the reader grounded in the scene. See how many references to time are included in the excerpt above:

- <u>On the evening of July 5</u> . . .

- . . . <u>after</u> having steered <u>all day</u> over a lumpy sea . . .

- I was afforded a look at the sun <u>just as</u> it was touching the sea.

- <u>Then</u> I turned my face eastward . . .

- Many a long talk <u>since then</u> I have had . . .

- <u>About midnight</u> the fog shut down again . . .

- It continued so <u>for a number of days</u> . . .

- <u>During these days</u> a feeling of awe . . .

Descriptive Details and Sensory Language

Descriptive details and sensory language can help a writer convey the setting and weather of a scene, tell about the narrator's activities, or reveal the narrator's feelings. In the excerpt above, look especially at how Slocum uses analogy and metaphor to describe the denseness of the fog and the intensity of his loneliness.

> *About midnight the fog shut down again denser than ever before. One could almost "stand on it." It continued so for a number of days, the wind increasing to a gale. The waves rose high, but I had a good ship. Still, in the dismal fog I felt myself drifting into loneliness, an insect on a straw in the midst of the elements. I lashed the helm, and my vessel held her course, and while she sailed I slept.*

Practice 1: Reflecting on Descriptive Details and Sensory Language

Reread the excerpt from Slocum's memoir. Underline any sentences that seem especially vivid to you. Choose one, and in the space below, explain what aspect of the language makes the description seem especially vivid. For example, does the sentence include an analogy or metaphor? Is there a word or phrase that creates an especially clear picture?

Dialogue

This excerpt includes some dialogue, even though the narrator is completely alone! Notice the difference that including bits of dialogue makes. The narrator could have simply said, *I talked to the moon.* But instead, he tells us exactly how he talked to the moon: *"Good evening, sir," I cried; "I'm glad to see you."*

Practice 2: Using Narrative Techniques

Try using some of the narrative techniques exemplified and explained above. Freewrite for five minutes on the topic of what you are doing right now. Where are you? What's the weather? How does your body feel? What's on your mind? If you pay attention and really focus on (for example) using descriptive details and sensory language, you might be surprised by how much you can say and how vividly you can write about just this moment.

_____

_____

_____

_____

_____

_____

_____

_____

_____

_____

_____

_____

_____

_____

_____

_____

_____

_____

_____

_____

_____

15

Writing a Strong Conclusion

Say all you have to say in the fewest possible words, or your reader will be sure to skip them; and in the plainest possible words or he will certainly misunderstand them.
—JOHN RUSKIN (1819–1900),
BRITISH ART CRITIC

Just as there are strategies for writing attention-getting beginnings, so are there strategies for writing thought-provoking conclusions. In this lesson, we'll take a look at these strategies. Concluding your essay or narrative is the focus of Standards **W.6.1e**, **W.6.2f**, **W.6.3e**, **W.7.1e**, **W.7.2f**, **W.7.3e**, **W.8.1e**, **W.8.2f**, and **W.8.3e**.

Writing a strong conclusion is as important as writing a strong introduction. An effective conclusion leaves readers not just with a good impression but with a lasting impression. Like an effective introduction, it sums up your ideas on a topic. It also leaves readers thinking about your topic.

Six Strategies for Concluding an Essay

The structure of the conclusion to an essay may be looser than that of its introduction. Generally, it should include a transition from the previous paragraph and sum up what the reader should have learned from the body of the essay. Finally, it should leave your reader with something to think about.

Sounds like a difficult feat to pull off? Luckily, there are specific strategies you can try.

1. **Summarize your ideas about the topic of the text with language that is memorable.** Let's say you're writing an essay about the value of standardized tests. You could conclude the essay by drawing attention to the implications of the word standardized.

    In short, standardized testing is based on the assumption that the results of education should be exactly the same for every single individual—standardized.

2. **Connect the topic of the text to a current trend or an idea that might be personally relevant to the reader.** This strategy helps your reader see how your topic and conclusions are meaningful to his or her life.

    In fact, well-organized boycotts of standardized tests have become common in communities throughout the nation. Given the opportunity to opt out, what would you do?

3. **Ask a question.** Notice that the previous example concluded with a question. Here's another one.

    Can we be sure that, at the very least, these tests are providing valuable information?

4. **Discuss the broader implications of the topic.** For instance, the following example connects concerns about the purposes of standardized tests with their costs. (Compare this example with the previous one.)

    Given the time that students spend on these tests and their cost in dollars to state and local governments, we need to be sure that, at the very least, these tests are providing valuable information.

Also, in discussing the implications of the topic, you may make a prediction.

Standardized tests have been a part of the American education system since the 1970s. Thus, for better or for worse, it seems they're here to stay.

See how the next example builds on this prediction.

5. **Suggest a solution to a problem or an action that could be taken.** Any solution you suggest should be realistic. Similarly, any call to action should be something that readers can do and might be willing to do. It should also be compelling—that is, an action that is likely to be effective.

Standardized tests have been a part of the American education system since the 1970s. Thus, for better or for worse, it seems they're here to stay. Therefore, while policymakers, educators, parents, and students argue about the value and purposes of these tests, you have another responsibility. Your task is to decide what your education is for and how your performance on a standardized test fits into it. In other words, set your own purpose for learning.

6. **Include a quotation that casts a new light on the topic.**

In a recent article published in The Atlantic, *Laura McKenna says that "education leaders should also answer the 'why?' question: Why should students take standardized tests?" Although generations of American students have taken these tests, the answer to this question remains incomplete.*

. . . .

TIP: Don't begin your conclusion with such clichéd or trite phrases as *In conclusion . . .* , *To summarize . . .* , *I conclude by . . .* , or *And so we see that. . . .* Furthermore, be sure not to repeat your thesis statement exactly as you presented it in the introduction. After all, by the time your reader finishes your essay, he or she should have more insight into your thesis. Your conclusion should reflect this additional insight.

. . . .

Practice 1: Drafting a Conclusion

Look back at the rough outline you wrote for practice in Lesson 13 (for an essay about a favorite movie). Choose one of the strategies discussed in this lesson, and draft a conclusion for this essay.

Concluding a Narrative

_____

_____

_____

_____

_____

_____

_____

_____

_____

The conclusion of a narrative is another opportunity to reveal what the experience meant to you or your characters. Some ways to conclude a personal narrative include the following:

- Tell how you felt about the experience at the time.

- Tell how you feel about the experience now.

- Reflect on the difference between your feelings then and your feelings now.

- Reflect on what you learned from the experience or how it changed you or your life.

- Echo an image or idea from the beginning of the narrative.

The conclusion of a fictional narrative might sum up the story, or give some variation on ". . . and they lived happily ever after." (In the last sentence of Jane Austen's *Sense and Sensibility*, the narrator concludes that "among the merits and the happiness of Elinor and Marianne, let it not be ranked as the least considerable, that though sisters, and living almost within sight of each other, they could live without disagreement between themselves, or producing coolness between their husbands.") A more common technique in contemporary literature is to conclude with one final, revealing scene. Reading widely is the best way to get ideas on how to conclude your own stories.

Practice 2: Reflecting on a Conclusion

Read the final paragraphs of Joshua Slocum's memoir, *Sailing Alone Around the World*. Identify two ways in which he reveals what his experience of sailing alone around the world meant to him. The *Spray*, you may recall, was his ship.

> If the Spray *discovered no continents on her voyage, it may be that there were no more continents to be discovered; she did not seek new worlds, or sail to powwow about the dangers of the seas. The sea has been much maligned. To find one's way to lands already discovered is a good thing, and the* Spray *made the discovery that even the worst sea is not so terrible to a well-appointed ship. No king, no country, no treasury at all, was taxed for the voyage of the* Spray, *and she accomplished all that she undertook to do.*
>
> *To succeed, however, in anything at all, one should go understandingly about his work and be prepared for every emergency. I see, as I look back over my own small achievement, a kit of not too elaborate carpenters' tools, a tin clock, and some carpet-tacks, not a great many, to facilitate the enterprise as already mentioned in the story. But above all to be taken into account were some years of schooling, where I studied with diligence Neptune's laws, and these laws I tried to obey when I sailed overseas; it was worth the while.*
>
> *And now, without having wearied my friends, I hope, with detailed scientific accounts, theories, or deductions, I will only say that I have endeav-*

ored to tell just the story of the adventure itself. This, in my own poor way, having been done, I now moor ship, weather-bitt cables, and leave the sloop Spray, *for the present, safe in port.*

1. _____

2. _____

Section 4

Revising and Editing Your Writing

After you've finished your rough draft, you can breathe a sigh of relief. You've done the work of transforming what may initially have seemed like a jumble of hard-to-capture ideas into language on the page. Now it's time to take a hard look at what you've written so that you can work some more transformations—this time, the transformations that will turn your rough draft into a gleamingly well-polished composition. In this section, we'll give you guidance on how to make this happen.

16

Revising Your Writing

Rewriting is the essence of writing well—where the game is won or lost.
—WILLIAM ZINSSER (1922–2015),
AMERICAN JOURNALIST, NONFICTION WRITER, AND TEACHER

Revising your writing is the first step of transforming your rough draft into a final composition. Revision, rewriting, and trying a new approach are all steps of the writing process outlined in Anchor Standard for Writing 5.

In Sections 1 and 2, you learned about prewriting. In Section 3, we walked you through the process of writing a first draft. Even after the work of prewriting, your first draft of a composition might be really rough. But as long as you have enough time to take a draft through the remaining stages of the writing process, there's no need to worry.

These remaining stages involve revising, editing, and proofreading your composition.

- During the **revising** stage, you focus on the big picture: the organization and development of your ideas, both overall and within each paragraph. This stage is the time to make substantial changes or improvements to your composition.

- During the **editing** stage, your focus narrows. This stage is the time to consider the tone of your composition, as well as sentence structure and your choice of words.

- During the **proofreading** stage, you attend to the details, checking for and correcting any errors in language use, spelling, and punctuation.

The focus of this lesson, of course, is revision. First, we'll give you an overview of the revision process. Then, we'll give you some checklists that you can use to review and revise an essay or narrative.

The Revision Process

Most writers will tell you that the process of revision is where the real work of writing takes place. *Revise* literally means "to see again." In practical terms, revision involves thinking critically about the content of your writing and how you have presented it. The process of revision involves much, much more than just fixing spelling and punctuation (which actually is a part of *proofreading* your writing, not revising it—see above!). When revising, you might rewrite, replace, or simply throw out entire sentences, paragraphs, or even pages of your writing. Your goal is to make sure not only that your writing actually says what you want it to say but also that readers will understand what you are saying.

. . . .

TIP: The later stages of the writing process don't always progress in a linear fashion. For example, while you are editing, you might decide to move a paragraph from the beginning to the end of your composition. Or while proofreading, you might make changes to improve the tone. Nevertheless, it can be useful to think of yourself as moving your composition through these steps.

. . . .

Whether you're revising an essay or a narrative, the very first thing to do is put away your first draft! Give yourself some time to get a fresh perspective on it. After several hours or (even better!) a day have passed, take another look. Here's what to do:

- Reread your draft while asking critical questions about your writing. While reviewing an essay, you might ask: Does the text have a clear focus? Have I supported my thesis and developed my ideas? While reviewing a narrative, you might ask: Is my story told clearly and in an engaging way? Has the meaning or importance of the story been revealed?

- Work on a paper copy of the text, so you can take notes as you reread. In your notes, suggest where more information is needed. Note which sentences or paragraphs could be rewritten, moved, or deleted. Jot down your ideas for rewrites.

- If possible, ask someone else to read your draft. General feedback, such as "It's great!" or "I don't get it," is not likely to help you. Therefore, ask your reader to respond to one or two critical questions about the draft. If your reader is given a specific question to answer, such as whether or not the organization of the draft makes sense, he or she is more likely to respond with helpful feedback.

- Using your notes and any feedback you received, write a new draft. Then, put this second draft away, and look at it later with a fresh perspective. You may find that there's more you want to change. Indeed, it may take several drafts to complete your composition.

Remember that the necessity of revision can free you of the burden of trying to get it right the first time. In each draft, you are free to write too much, say things badly, make mistakes, and get messy. Just be sure to give yourself plenty of time to clean up the mess!

Checklists for Revising an Essay

To be a good critic of your own writing, you need to ask critical questions like those provided in the following checklists. First, take a step back to look at the big picture. Use the questions in the first checklist to consider the overall focus and organization of your essay. Based on your answers to these questions, you might write a second draft of your essay. Next, take a closer look. Use the questions in the second checklist to consider each paragraph in your essay.

A Checklist for Considering the Overall Focus and Organization of an Essay

- Is your thesis or overall topic so broad that you cannot cover it all? Are you finding that you have no room to explore ideas with any depth or detail? Are you having to leave out important ideas? If so, you might need to make your thesis more specific.

- Is your thesis or overall topic so narrow that you don't have much to say? Are you repeating yourself in order to fill space? If so, you might need to expand the scope of your thesis.

- Does your thesis still reflect what you really think? If your ideas have changed, you might need to revise or replace your thesis so that it better matches your new ideas.

- Does the thesis clearly relate to all of the information given to support it? If not, you might need to revise your thesis so that it reflects the information presented in the body of the text. Or you might need to revise your body paragraphs—or even get rid of one or more of them—so that they all clearly reflect your thesis.

- Finally, does the sequence of topics make sense? In other words, is information presented in a logical pattern, such as chronologically or according to subtopic? If not, you might need to arrange your body paragraphs in a different order, move information from one paragraph to another, or combine or divide paragraphs.

A Checklist for Considering Individual Paragraphs

- Does each body paragraph have a clear topic sentence? Underline or highlight this sentence.

- Is the idea in the topic sentence fully supported and explained in the paragraph? What, if anything, might need to be added or explained further?

- Does all of the information in the paragraph relate to the idea in the topic sentence? If some of the information doesn't belong in the paragraph, should it be moved to another paragraph, made into a new paragraph of its own, or deleted altogether?

- Finally, introductory and concluding paragraphs deserve special consideration. Ask yourself whether they clearly introduce and wrap up your ideas and also whether they draw readers in and leave them thinking about your ideas.

Practice 1: Revising a Paragraph

Here is a paragraph that a student wrote to support the thesis *The eating habits of students throughout the country are leading to serious health hazards.*

> *In their rush to get out the door and to school on time, kids today are very likely to skip breakfast, and that's the worst possible way to start your day. Even a quick bowl of cereal will make all the difference between a healthy start to the day and a long, sleepy morning.*

Using the checklists above, evaluate this paragraph. Write two ways that the student could improve it.

1. _____

   _____

2. _____

   _____

Checklists for Revising a Narrative

The critical questions to ask about a narrative are somewhat different from those you would ask about an essay. These questions help you see whether you have fulfilled the particular purposes of a narrative: first, to make the story come alive for your readers; and second, to reveal its significance.

A Checklist: Have You Made the Story Come Alive?

- Does the beginning of the narrative include ideas and details that give readers context for understanding the story? Are the ideas and details interesting and vivid and therefore likely to get readers curious about your story?

- Does the narrative tell about events in the order in which they happened? Does the sequence of events make sense?

- Does the narrative include transitions and words about space and time to help readers understand where and when specific events and actions took place?

- Have you used narrative techniques such as description and dialogue to show the setting, characters, and events, rather than just tell readers about them?

A Checklist: Have You Revealed the Significance of the Story?

- Do the descriptions, dialogue, and scenes in the narrative show the narrator's thoughts and feelings about the setting, characters, and events?

- Does the conclusion of the narrative include reflections on the meaning or importance of the experience to the narrator? Does the conclusion feel like it follows naturally from the rest of the narrative, or does it feel like a lesson that has been tacked on to the end as an afterthought?

Practice 2: Revising a Narrative

Here is a 205-word rough draft of a narrative that a student wrote about coming to love a favorite place:

> *When my mom first got her big-city job, we were excited about our big move from the suburbs. But Brooklyn turned out to be noisier and dirtier than I expected. Everywhere I looked, I saw asphalt, concrete, and brick. Luckily, Brooklyn has Prospect Park, too.*
>
> *The day I first set foot in the park was not its prettiest day. Clouds hung low in the sky, as though it was about to rain or snow. The leaves were long gone, and so were the holidays. As I always do in February, I longed for spring.*
>
> *It was our first weekend in our new home, and my mom could see that I was lonely. "Let's take Elmo for a walk," she suggested. Elmo is our dog.*
>
> *Once we got to the park, I was amazed. I saw so many people running, biking, tossing footballs back and forth, and walking their dogs. The cold didn't matter at all, because all these people (and their dogs, too) were filling the park with their energy. I also got excited thinking about how beautiful the park would be when spring arrived with leaves and new grass.*
>
> *Some people prefer the beach, but for me, Prospect Park is the place to be!*

The assignment requires the student to write 400–500 words, so she needs to develop this narrative further. Using the checklists above, evaluate the narrative. Write two ways that the student could improve it.

1. _____

   _____

   _____

2. _____

   _____

   _____

17

Editing Your Writing: Habits to Avoid

Vigorous writing is concise. A sentence should contain no unnecessary words, a paragraph no unnecessary sentences, for the same reason that a drawing should have no unnecessary lines and a machine no unnecessary parts.
—WILLIAM STRUNK, JR. (1869–1946),
AMERICAN EDITOR AND WRITER

During the editing stage, your focus narrows. Your concerns include your choice of words, as outlined in Standard **L.7.3a**, and the style and tone of your writing, as outlined in Standards **W.6.1d**, **W.7.1d**, **W.8.1d**, **W.6.2e**, **W.7.2e**, **W.8.2e**, and **L.6.3b**.

As you become satisfied with the organization and development of your composition, your focus will turn to its language. In this lesson, we'll look at some ways of using language that should be avoided. Keep in mind that the more you write, the greater ease you'll have using language overall and the more likely you'll follow these guidelines naturally. But if poor wording does creep in, you can fix it during the editing process.

1. Avoid Wordiness

To write clearly, avoid using unnecessary words. This is not to say that long sentences are bad, or that shorter is always better. After all, you need words to get your ideas across! You just don't want to clutter up your writing with extra words that get in the way of your meaning. Compare the following examples:

> *The students in my class at school on Friday were in an uproar and complaining on account of the fact that our teacher had not been exactly cool and had given them an assignment to write an essay over the weekend.*

> *The students in my class were in an uproar because our teacher had assigned an essay to write over the weekend.*

The extra words in the first example might have helped the writer meet a word-count requirement, but they also make the writing seem sloppy and unclear.

    Here are some tips for avoiding this problem:

- **Eliminate filler language.** Many common phrases add little meaning to your writing and can easily be cut. In the examples above, notice that the seven words *on the account of the fact that* can be replaced with one: *because.*

- **Eliminate redundant words.** If the sentence already says that the students "were in an uproar," it doesn't also need to say that they were "complaining."

- **Eliminate unnecessary adjectives and adverbs.** In the example above, is it necessary to describe the teacher as "not exactly cool"? In particular, note that modifiers like *very*, *so*, or (as in the example above) *exactly* can almost always be eliminated. For example, instead of "The man was very tall," write, "The man was tall."

- **Avoid long strings of prepositional phrases.** A series of three or more prepositional phrases can be disorienting for the reader. Try to eliminate some of them. (See Lesson 23 for a description of prepositional phrases.)

2. Avoid Clichés and Slang

Have a nice day. Trust me. No problem. These are examples of **clichés**—phrases that have been so overused that they may sap energy from your writing. Similarly, the use of **slang**, or informal language, can undermine the authority of your writing. Compare the following examples:

> *Homework over the weekend is totally a bummer.*

> *Writing an essay is not the activity I would choose to do on a Saturday night.*

Both sentences convey the same idea, but the first example is slack and lacks authority. The second example, on the other hand, is vivid and credible.

In an essay, maintaining a formal style and tone is especially crucial. You want your audience to take you and your ideas seriously. If you're writing a narrative, however, it may be appropriate to use a less formal tone. Consider your audience and purpose. For example, is your purpose to win over your readers by getting them to laugh? Or is your purpose to reveal the character of your first-person narrator? In cases like these, a casual, conversational tone is likely to be appropriate.

. . . .

TIP: In order to maintain the appearance of objectivity, writers often exclude the first-person pronouns (*I, me, my, mine, myself*) from their formal writing, such as arguments and informational texts. In recent decades, though, many nonfiction writers, including journalists, have used the first person more freely. They have a particular point of view on their subject, and they don't want to pretend to be objective.

What about you—when should you use the first-person pronouns in an argument or informational text? When you're writing for a school assignment, check the assignment or with your teacher. Or to get your own sense of when to use first person, look through all of the articles in a newspaper. Which types of articles include the first person? Which do not? What is the effect?

. . . .

3. Don't Go to the Thesaurus to Find Impressive Words

Although you certainly want to avoid language that is too casual for your purpose, resist the temptation to dress up your language with words you find in the thesaurus. As Stephen King, one the country's most successful writers, says, "any word you have to hunt for in a thesaurus is the wrong word. There are no exceptions to this rule." The big words you find in a thesaurus are likely to come across as awkward and unsuitable—and you are likely to come across as foolish and insecure. Rely on vivid and exact words to get your ideas across; these will most often be the simplest words.

What do we mean by "vivid and exact words"? Read on. . . .

4. Avoid Vague Language

Vague language often reflects vague thinking. To address this problem, pay special attention to the nouns and verbs you've used; these form the foundation of each sentence in your composition. The best nouns are exact, and the best verbs are vivid and strong. For example, consider the following sentence:

> *The tall, large, yellow-petaled flowers were in front.*

This sentence is O.K., but if it included exact nouns and strong verbs, it could be better. For example, instead of describing the flowers, why not name the flowers with an exact noun, like *sunflowers*? And instead of using a linking verb like *were*, why not use a verb that stands for an action, like *stood*?

> *The sunflowers stood in front.*

This sentence is better. But an even more vivid verb could be used to show that the sunflowers were tall. And other exact nouns could be added to show exactly where the flowers stood.

The sunflowers towered above the other flowers in the front garden.

When you edit your writing, look out for adverbs. In many cases, an adverb can be eliminated if a stronger verb is used. For example, compare the following two sentences:

The children quickly ran outside.

The children dashed outside.

Rather than dress up the plain verb *ran* with the adverb *quickly*, you can get your same point across by using a single, more meaningful verb: *dashed.*

Practice 1: Editing a Paragraph

Here is a paragraph that a student wrote to support the thesis *Today's astronomical tools are introducing us to new mysteries in the universe, even while they help us solve others.*

One inscrutability of the universe is actually literally completely invisible, so much so that it is actually called "dark energy." It's this stuff that scientists can't really see. They think it's out there, because the augmentation of the universe is getting faster instead of slower, which it should be doing because of the fact of gravity. They came up with the idea of dark energy to explain the speedy expansion of space, but no one knows what it really is or can see it. In fact it is true that all the stuff we can see, including stars, planets, and everything else, makes up only 5% of the matter and energy that's out there. I think this is totally awesome, and you should, too.

Edit this paragraph to eliminate wordiness, clichés and slang, unsuitable words that may have been taken from a thesaurus, and vague language. Rewrite the paragraph below.

_____

_____

_____

_____

_____

_____

_____

_____

_____

_____

_____

_____

_____

_____

_____

_____

_____

_____

_____

_____

18
Editing Your Writing: Habits to Adopt

Style is an increment in writing. . . . Every writer, by the way he uses language, reveals something of his spirit, his habits, his capacities, his bias. This is inevitable, as well as enjoyable. All writing is communication; creative writing is communication through revelation—it is the Self escaping into the open. No writer long remains incognito.
—E. B. WHITE (1899–1985),
AMERICAN WRITER

In this lesson, we continue our overview of editing, when your focus is on the tone of your composition, as well as sentence structure and your choice of words. We'll look at domain-specific vocabulary, as outlined in Standards **W.6.2d**, **W.7.2d**, and **W.8.2d**; transitional words and phrases, as outlined in Standards **W.6.1c**, **W.6.2c**, **W.7.1c**, **W.7.2c**, **W.8.1c**, and **W.8.2c**; and varying sentence structures, as outlined in Standard **L.6.3a**. We'll also look at some of the ways you can format your composition, as outlined in Standards **W.6.2a**, **W.7.2a**, and **W.8.2a**.

The previous lesson gave an overview of some writing habits to avoid. In this lesson, we'll look at some writing habits to adopt. These can be incorporated into your writing during the editing process.

1. Use Domain-Specific Vocabulary

Domain-specific vocabulary is just a fancy term for words that are specific to a particular subject area. These are words that you see in your textbook and use in the classroom. Most are words that you don't frequently use in everyday life.

Here are some examples:

- **from mathematics:** *congruence, polygon, prime factor*

- **from science:** *atom, cell, ecosystem, vertebrate*

- **from history:** *civil disobedience, emigration, tariffs*

- **from geography:** *hemisphere, natural resource, population density*

Using domain-specific vocabulary serves a few purposes. For example, these words can help you keep your writing concise (not wordy) and precise (not vague). Consider the following examples:

> *The only reason that the northern part of the world almost always appears at the top of a map is because that's just what's been done for centuries.*

> *The Northern Hemisphere appears at the top of most maps only because of custom.*

See how using terms from geography and social studies results in a more concise, precise sentence? Also notice the more formal tone of the second sentence. Using language that is particular to a subject area shows that you have authority on the subject.

2. Use Transitions

Using transition words and phrases doesn't just improve the flow of your writing. It also helps you show the relationships between the ideas and events in your essay or narrative. Transition words and phrases can help you highlight cause-and-effect relationships, sequences of events, comparisons and contrasts, and so on. For example:

- To show the similarity between ideas, use *also, likewise,* or *similarly.*

- To contrast ideas, use *but, however, one the one hand . . . on the other hand, nevertheless, in contrast, still,* or *yet.*

- To show sequence, use *first, second, third, next, then,* or *finally.*

- To show time order, use *after, afterward, at last, before, currently, during, earlier, immediately, later, meanwhile, now, recently,* or *then.*

- To show cause-and-effect relationships, use consequently, *so, therefore,* or *thus.*

- To introduce examples, use *for example, for instance,* or *such as.*

- To give additional support, use *additionally, also, and, further, furthermore, in addition, moreover,* or *then.*

- To emphasize an idea, use *after all, indeed, in fact,* or *of course.*

- To conclude or summarize ideas, use *finally, in conclusion, in the end, thus, to conclude, to summarize, to sum up,* or *in summary.*

Compare the following two paragraphs:

In the U.S., gray whales are no longer officially listed as an endangered species. A population that migrates between the Arctic and Mexico along the coast of California is thriving. A population that lives in the western Pacific is not doing well. Another population that once lived in the Atlantic is now gone.

In the U.S., gray whales are no longer officially listed as an endangered species. Indeed, a population that migrates between the Arctic and Mexico along the coast of California is thriving. <u>However</u>, a population that lives in the western Pacific is not doing well. <u>Additionally</u>, another population that once lived in the Atlantic is now gone.

Source: "Gray whale" in Britannica Library Reference Center, accessed via the Brooklyn Public Library

Do you see how much clearer the second paragraph is? The transitions help to show whether a sentence adds to the information given previously or introduces a contrasting idea.

3. Vary Your Sentence Structure

Too often writers get stuck on a sentence-structure treadmill. They adopt a sentence pattern and repeat is over and over again. Usually this pattern is *noun → verb → object*. While there's certainly nothing wrong with this sentence structure in itself, it gets boring if repeated too often. Varying your sentence structure results in a more varied rhythm, which keeps readers interested. Notice the difference in the rhythm of these two passages:

> Writing is not my favorite subject. The lessons are difficult to learn. Reading about writing helps. The rules are easy enough to understand. Using them is a different story.

> To say the least, writing is not my favorite subject. I find that reading about writing helps, but the lessons are difficult to learn. While the rules are easy enough to understand, learning how to use them is quite a different story.

The rhythm of the first passage is much choppier. Furthermore, the repeated sentence structure gives every idea equal weight. Notice that in the second passage, related ideas are joined in sentences. The structure of the sentences beginning with "I find that . . ." and "While the rules . . ." highlights the contradictions that the author experiences while learning about writing. (For descriptions of different types of sentences, see Lesson 23.)

4. Use Text Features to Organize Information

In informational texts, using text features can help you organize information. Text features are all those elements of a text that are not part of the main body of the text. Text features you might use include the following:

- **Headings** can be used to identify the topic of each section of a longer text.

- **Bulleted lists** (such as this one!) can be used to highlight lists of similar items or ideas.

- **Labels** can be used to identify any graphic features included in your text, such as illustrations, while **captions** can be used to give more information about these graphic features.

- **Sidebars** can be used to give information that relates to the topic of your text but does not belong in the main body of the text.

· ·

TIP: How can text features help you organize information? Just look at how we've used them to organize the information in this book! Headings clearly identify the topic of each section of every lesson. Bulleted and numbered lists arrange what otherwise might seem like disparate ideas in an orderly way. And sidebars like this one call out handy tips!

· ·

Practice 1: Editing a Paragraph

Here is a paragraph that a student wrote to support the thesis *Ideas about what makes good art change frequently*.

> *The Rite of Spring* is a piece of music by Igor Stravinsky. He wrote it for a ballet. The ballet was first performed in 1913. It was performed in Paris. No one had ever heard music like it before. To their ears, the sounds of the notes seemed to clash. The beats seemed loud and barbaric. The people listening and watching behaved badly. They argued with each other. They argued loudly. The dancers couldn't hear the music. The police even came. There were no riots at any of the remaining performances of the ballet. Today, *The Rite of Spring* is seen as a masterpiece of 20th-century music.

Edit this paragraph to add transitions and variety to the sentences. Use domain-specific vocabulary as appropriate, including such words as *harmonies*, *rhythms*, and *audience*. Add a heading, and rewrite the paragraph below.

_____

_____

_____

_____

_____

_____

_____

_____

_____

_____

_____

_____

_____

_____

_____

_____

_____

_____

_____

_____

_____

_____

Section 5

A Review of the Conventions of Standard English

Maybe you think of yourself as "having good grammar" or "having bad grammar"; if so, do your best to forget about these ideas. We study the structure of our language so that we can use it effectively. Therefore, our aim in this section of the book is not to learn rules so that we can write correct sentences. Instead, our aim is to come to an understanding of how the English language works—particularly how the written language works—so that we can use it effectively.

19

The Big Four Parts of Speech

*Writing is an exploration. You start
from nothing and learn as you go.*
—E. L. Doctorow (1931–2015),
American novelist

In this lesson, we'll review the uses of nouns, adjectives, verbs, and adverbs. Understanding and applying the conventions of standard English is the focus of Anchor Standards for Language 1 and 3.

Each of the words in a sentence has a specific function, or job. Some words tell who or what the sentence is about. Some words express actions or states of being. Other words tell where or how. These functions of words are categorized in eight parts of speech. We'll begin our study of language use by reviewing four of these parts of speech: nouns, adjectives, verbs, and adverbs.

Nouns

Nouns name persons, places, things, and states or qualities.

- **persons:** *boy*, *Fred*

- **places:** *city*, *New York City*

- **things:** *window*, *ocean*

- **states or qualities:** *joy*, *wealth*

The list above includes both **common nouns**, such as *boy* and *city*, and **proper nouns**, such as *Fred* and *New York City*. A proper noun names a specific person, place, or thing and is capitalized. Notice the difference in the following sentences:

> *Latoya visited the White House.*

> *Latoya visited the white house.*

In the first example, *the White House* refers to a specific place: the home of the president of the United States. In the second example, *the white house* refers simply to a house that is painted white.

A noun may function as the subject of a sentence or as the object of a verb or preposition. In the following sentence, the nouns are underlined:

> *During her <u>trip</u>, <u>Latoya</u> visited the <u>White House</u>.*

In this sentence, *Latoya* is the subject. The sentence is about her. *White House* is the object of the verb *visited*. It tells what Latoya visited. And *trip* is the object of the preposition *during*. It helps to tell when Latoya visited the White House.

Practice 1: Identifying and Correcting Nouns

Identify and underline each noun in the following sentences. If necessary, correct its capitalization.

1. King kong was taken from the jungle to New york city where he eventually met a sad end.
2. Probably the most famous duck in the world is named Donald duck.
3. Thousands of nervous High School Students across america compete to become students at a prestigious University named princeton.
4. The small herd of buffalos in San francisco's golden gate park is a popular tourist Attraction.
5. At home, do you mostly speak English or your native Language, creole?

Adjectives

Adjectives modify nouns. In other words, they describe, specify, or qualify. For example, identify the adjectives in the following phrases:

> *cool group*
> *boring lesson*
> *patient teacher*
> *interesting book*

In these phrases, *cool*, *boring*, *patient*, and *interesting* are adjectives. They describe the group, lesson, teacher, and book. Not all adjectives are so descriptive or vivid, though; remember, adjectives specify and qualify as well as describe. For example, the articles *a*, *an*, and *the* are categorized as adjectives. And consider the underlined adjectives in the following phrases:

> <u>*that*</u> *girl*
> <u>*every*</u> *student*
> <u>*another*</u> *day*

Practice 2: Identifying Adjectives

Return to the five sentences in Practice 1, and now circle the adjectives in each sentence. Don't worry about the articles *a*, *an*, and *the*.

· ·

TIP: Many, many words can be used as more than one part of speech. Whether a word is a noun or an adjective, for example, depends on the context of the sentence. *High school* is typically a noun, and you might have identified it as a noun in sentence 3 of Practice 1. But in that sentence, it's really being used as an adjective, modifying *students*. Similarly, do you see that the possessive pronoun *your* in sentence 5 is being used as an adjective?

· ·

Verbs

Verbs express action or states of being. **Action verbs** tell what the subject is (or was or will be) doing.

> *Joseph <u>smiles</u>.*
> *We <u>wanted</u> a vacation.*
> *I <u>will see</u> that movie tomorrow.*

Linking verbs simply tell what the subject is (or was or will be).

> *Joseph <u>is</u> my brother.*
> *We <u>seemed</u> tired.*
> *I <u>will be</u> so happy!*

The verb *be* is the most common linking verb. Forms of this verb appear in the first (*is*) and third (*will be*) sentences above.

Practice 3: Identifying Verbs

Identify and underline each verb in the following sentences. (Be careful: watch out for verbs that are acting as nouns or adjectives. These are called verbals. We'll study verbals in Lesson 22.)

1. The dogs barked furiously as the cars frantically whizzed past on their way to the rock concert that will begin at midnight.
2. I laughed uproariously when I realized how nervous I had been about doing well on the geography test.
3. More than two dozen species of animals peacefully inhabit the wildlife preserve.
4. Trudging wearily through a driving snow to school every day used to be a common event in some parts of the Midwest.
5. Prince, whose original name was Prince Rogers Nelson, famously began his musical career during junior high school with a small band called Grand Central.

Adverbs

Adverbs are words that modify a verb, an adjective, or another adverb. For example, identify the adverbs in the following phrases:

> singing badly
> carefully picking blackberries
> sleeping soundly
> write easily
> vigorously competing to win
> gratefully counting blessings

Practice 4: Identifying Adverbs

Return to the five sentences in Practice 3, and now circle the adverbs in each sentence.

Answers

Practice 1: Identifying and Correcting Nouns and Practice 2: Identifying Adjectives

1. <u>King Kong</u> was taken from the <u>jungle</u> to <u>New York City</u> where he eventually met a (sad) <u>end</u>.

2. Probably the most (famous) <u>duck</u> in the <u>world</u> is named <u>Donald Duck</u>.

3. Thousands of (nervous) (high school) <u>students</u> across <u>America</u> compete to become <u>students</u> at a (prestigious) <u>university</u> named <u>Princeton</u>.

4. The (small) <u>herd</u> of <u>buffalos</u> in <u>San Francisco's</u> <u>Golden Gate Park</u> is a (popular) (tourist) <u>attraction</u>.

5. At <u>home</u>, do you mostly speak <u>English</u> or (your) (native) <u>language</u>, <u>Creole</u>?

Practice 3: Identifying Verbs and Practice 4: Identifying Adverbs

1. The dogs <u>barked</u> (furiously) as the cars (frantically) <u>whizzed</u> (past) on their way to the rock concert that <u>will begin</u> at midnight.

2. I <u>laughed</u> (uproariously) when I <u>realized</u> how nervous I <u>had been</u> about doing (well) on the geography test.

3. More than two dozen species of animals (peacefully) <u>inhabit</u> the wildlife preserve.

4. Trudging (wearily) through a driving snow to school (every day) <u>used to be</u> a common event in some parts of the Midwest.

5. Prince, whose original name <u>was</u> Prince Rogers Nelson, (famously) <u>began</u> his musical career during junior high school with a small band called Grand Central.

20

Properties of Verbs

Poetry is all nouns and verbs.
—MARIANNE MOORE (1887–1972),
AMERICAN POET

In this lesson, we'll give special attention to two of the properties of verbs: voice and mood. These are the focus of Standards **L.8.1b**, **L.8.1c**, **L.8.1d**, and **L.8.3a**.

When used in a sentence, a verb has five properties, or qualities. These properties are as follows:

- **tense:** present, past, future, etc.

- **person:** first person, second person, or third person

- **number:** singular or plural

- **voice:** active or passive

- **mood:** indicative, imperative, interrogative, conditional, or subjunctive

You may be less familiar with voice and mood than with the other properties of verbs, so let's take a look at those.

Voice

In the **active voice**, the subject of the sentence is the agent. In other words, the subject does the action expressed by the verb. The following sentence is in the active voice:

> *Our teacher read this book.*

Our teacher is the subject of this sentence. The teacher did the action expressed by the verb: *read*.

In the **passive voice**, the subject of the sentence is not acting, but being acted on. In other words, the subject receives the action expressed by the verb. The following sentence is in the passive voice:

> *This book was read by our teacher.*

Book is the subject of this sentence. The book received the action expressed by the verb: it was read. Notice that in this sentence, the verb phrase begins with a helping verb, *was*. In the passive voice, the verb phrase includes a form of the verb be, such as *am*, *are*, *is*, *was*, *were*, or *been*. Also notice that in this sentence, the agent (*teacher*) is named in a prepositional phrase beginning with the preposition *by*. However, a sentence in the passive voice may or may not identify the agent.

Sentences in the passive voice are often awkward, unnecessarily lengthy, and even confusing. To change a sentence in the passive voice, first identify the agent, which may be named in a prepositional phrase beginning with *by*. Then make the agent the subject of the sentence and adjust the verb.

> **Passive voice:** *The vegetables were left uneaten by the children.*
> **Active voice:** *The children left the vegetables uneaten.*

There are a few cases in which it makes sense to use the passive voice. Sometimes, for example, the agent is unknown.

> *The book was left out in the rain.*

Notice that this sentence is mainly about the book and not about the unknown person who left it out in the rain. As in this example, the passive voice can help you emphasize the recipient of an action. The following are two more examples:

Hannah sulked all evening after she was cut from the varsity team.

We had no option left but to walk the entire way home.

The passive voice is used in the subordinate clause of the first sentence to maintain the emphasis on Hannah ("she"), who is the subject of the main clause. In the second sentence, the use of the passive voice emphasizes the helplessness of the *we*.

Practice 1: Identifying and Correcting Passive Voice

Two of the following three sentences are in passive voice. Identify and correct them.

1. When we returned home, our basement was found to be flooded.
2. I was paying attention in class but still had trouble with my math homework.
3. The baseball was hit into a corner of the park, and the batter made it safely home.

Mood

The common moods in the English language are the indicative, imperative, interrogative, conditional, and subjunctive.

Most sentences are in the **indicative mood**. They tell about what is real or is observed to be true.

Alfred goes back to school today.

Sentences in the **imperative mood** give commands. The subject (you) is typically not named in the sentence but is understood.

Go back to school!

Sentences in the **interrogative mood** pose questions.

> *Will Alfred go back to school today or tomorrow?*

The **conditional mood** is used to tell about situations that are dependent on hypothetical or otherwise unreal conditions. Hypothetical conditions are supposed or possible but not necessarily true. The modal verbs *would, could,* or *might* are used to express the conditional mood. The hypothetical or unreal condition is typically expressed in a clause beginning with such words as *if* or *unless*.

> *If Alfred feels well enough, he might go back to school today.*

> *If Alfred had felt well enough, he would have gone back to school today.*

In the first sentence, Alfred's feeling better is a hypothetical condition. It's possible, but not necessarily true. Therefore, the verb in the main clause is in the conditional mood (*might go*). In the second sentence, the condition described in the clause beginning with *if* is unreal. Alfred did not feel enough. The verb in the main clause is in the conditional mood (*would have gone*).

The conditional mood is often linked to the **subjunctive mood**. The subjunctive mood was once used more widely in English. Now it is used only to express conditions that are not true. It is used in clauses beginning with if and after verbs that express a wish. It is also used in subordinate clauses that express an order or recommendation, although as you can see from the third example that follows, this use of the subjunctive mood is uncommon enough to seem strange.

> *If Alfred were better, he would go to school.*

> *Alfred wishes that he were back at school.*

> *It is best that Alfred rest today.*

Practice 2: Identifying Mood

Match each sentence on the left with the description of its mood on the right.

To get to Boston by noon, take the train that leaves at 7:30.	Indicative
If I had more time, I would go to Boston this weekend.	Imperative
How I wish I were in Boston with you today!	Interrogative
When can I go to visit my cousin in Boston?	Conditional
Last year I went to Boston only once, in the fall.	Subjunctive

Answers

Practice 1: Identifying and Correcting Passive Voice

When we returned home, we found our basement flooded.

or

When we returned home, we found that our basement was flooded.

The batter hit the baseball into a corner of the park, and he made it safely home.

or

The batter hit the baseball into a corner of the park and made it safely home.

Practice 2: Identifying Mood

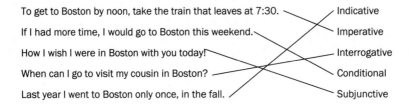

To get to Boston by noon, take the train that leaves at 7:30.   Indicative

If I had more time, I would go to Boston this weekend.   Imperative

How I wish I were in Boston with you today!   Interrogative

When can I go to visit my cousin in Boston?   Conditional

Last year I went to Boston only once, in the fall.   Subjunctive

21

The All-Important Pronouns

I love being a writer. What I can't stand is the paperwork.
—Peter De Vries (1910–1993),
American novelist

In this lesson, we'll review pronouns and how to use them most clearly and effectively. Pronouns and their use are the focus of Standards **L.6.1a**, **L.6.1b**, **L.6.1c**, and **L.6.1d**.

Pronouns may be little words, but (like many little children!) they can be troublesome. However, remember that you likely use them every day, all the time, without hesitation. If you give some thought to how they function in a sentence, you'll be able to use them clearly in your writing.

What Are Pronouns?

A **pronoun** takes the place of a noun (or noun phrase) in a sentence. Just imagine the English language without pronouns! Take a look at this sentence:

The girl visited a friend, who loaned the girl a book, and afterward the girl went home to do the girl's homework.

Here's the sentence again, with pronouns:

The girl visited a friend, who loaned her a book, and afterward she went home to do her homework.

The **antecedent** is the word or phrase that the pronoun replaces or refers to. In the sentence above, the antecedent of the pronouns *she* and *her* is *girl*.

Personal Pronouns

Personal pronouns may be what come to your mind first when you think about pronouns. This chart shows their forms, which vary according to person, number, and case.

SINGULAR PERSONAL PRONOUNS

	Subjective	Objective	Possessive
first person	I	me	my, mine
second person	you	you	your, yours
third person	he, she, it	him, her, it	his, her, hers, its

PLURAL PERSONAL PRONOUNS

	Subjective	Objective	Possessive
first person	we	us	our, ours
second person	you	you	your, yours
third person	they	them	their, theirs

- The **person** of a pronoun indicates whether the pronoun refers to the person speaking (first person), the person being spoken to (second person), or the person being spoken about (third person).

- The **number** of a pronoun indicates whether the pronoun refers to one person or thing (singular) or many (plural).

- The case of a pronoun indicates its function in a sentence.

Pronoun Case

The **subjective case** is used when the pronoun serves as the subject of the sentence.

She wrote another song last night.

The subjective case is also used with a linking verb, such as *is* in the following sentence:

The best player in the band is she.

This sentence might sound strange to you, and you might think you should change the *she* to *her*. But if you turn the sentence around, you'll see that *she* is indeed the pronoun that makes sense. "She is the best player in the band" sounds right, whereas "Her is the best player in the band" does not.

The **objective case** is used when the pronoun serves as the object of a verb or preposition.

Object of a verb: *Ms. Johnson asked her to play the song.*
Object of a preposition: *Ms. Johnson asked for everyone except for her to be quiet.*

The **possessive case** is used to indicate ownership. Possessive pronouns may be used as the subject, predicate nominative, or object. They are also often used as adjectives.

Subject: *Hers is the best song.*
Predicate nominative: *The best song is hers.*
Object: *Let's play that song after we listen to hers.*
Adjective: *I thought about her song all day.*

Practice 1: Choosing and Identifying Personal Pronouns

Choose the personal pronouns that best complete the following sentences. Identify each pronoun as subjective or objective. Circle the possessive pronouns.

1. Our science teacher, Ms. Gioia, beamed at Tom and (*I, me*).
2. The other kids in the class applauded, too, when (*he and I, him and me*) were awarded the prize.
3. Tom and (*I, me*) had worked for two months on our science project.
4. Ms. Gioia wanted to make an example of Tom, (*I, me*), and our work to the rest of the class, so (*we, us*) agreed to demonstrate our experiment.
5. Tom predicts that (*he and I, him and me*) will win the grand prize next year.

Reflexive and Intensive Pronouns

Reflexive and intensive pronouns all end in *–self* or *–selves*: *myself, yourself, himself, herself, itself, ourselves, yourselves, themselves.*

Reflexive pronouns refer to the subject of the sentence. They show the action of the sentence returning to the subject.

> *John Lennon dedicated himself to promoting world peace.*

> *Yoko Ono joined John and called herself a peace advocate.*

Intensive pronouns emphasize another pronoun or noun in the sentence.

> *The Beatles themselves wrote all of their own music.*

> *I myself have always been a devoted fan of Ringo.*

Whereas a reflexive pronoun is essential to the meaning of a sentence, an intensive pronoun is not.

Practice 2: Using Intensive Pronouns

Add an intensive pronoun to each of the following sentences.

1. The coach was shocked at her team's performance.
2. I scored the game-winning goal.
3. The season was otherwise unremarkable.

Relative and Interrogative Pronouns

The **relative pronouns** include *who, whom, whose, which,* and *that* as well as *whoever, whomever,* and *whichever.* These pronouns join dependent and independent clauses. They also join a clause with its antecedent. (A clause is a group of words that includes a subject and verb. We'll look more closely at dependent and independent clauses in Lesson 23.)

The following sentences include relative pronouns:

> *I will help whoever needs the most help.*

> *The novel that I finished last week is still giving me nightmares.*

Use the relative pronoun *that* when the clause it begins is essential to the meaning of the sentence. Use the pronoun *which* and a comma when the clause it begins is not essential to the overall meaning of the sentence. For example:

> *I enjoyed the novel that I finished last week much better than I'm enjoying this one.*

> *That novel, which I finished last week, is a terrifying ghost story.*

In the first sentence, the clause "that I finished last week" gives necessary information. It helps to distinguish one novel from another. *That* is used. In the second sentence, the clause "which I finished last week" gives extra information. It could be left out, and the sentence would still make sense. *Which* is used. (This clause is an example of a nonrestrictive element, which will come up again in Lesson 24.)

The **interrogative pronouns** are *who* (nominative), *whom* (objective), *whose* (possessive), *which*, and *what*. These pronouns are used in questions.

> *Whose books are these?*
> *Which book did you like better?*
> *What book did you leave at home?*

Although very few people use the pronoun *whom* when they're speaking, it is typically used in formal writing. *Who* is used as the subject of a question or relative clause, and whom is used as an object.

> *Who is planning to come to the party?*
> *The family who just moved in next door is coming.*
> *For whom did you buy this gift?*
> *The girl whom I just met would also like to join us.*

Practice 3: *That* or *Which*? *Who* or *Whom*?

Choose the pronoun that best completes each of the following sentences. If the pronoun you choose is *which*, then add a comma or commas as necessary.

1. The dress (*that, which*) I bought yesterday is the one I'm planning to wear.
2. Let's go to the restaurant (*that, which*) is opening tonight.
3. This gift (*that, which*) of course is just lovely is also unnecessary.
4. Please invite any friends (*who, whom*) you think will want to come.
5. I meant to ask the young man (*who, whom*) you greeted what his name was.
6. (*Who, Whom*) asked for more pizza?

Answers

Practice 1: Choosing and Identifying Personal Pronouns

1. me (objective)
2. he and I (subjective)
3. I (subjective)
4. me (objective), we (subjective)
5. he and I (subjective)

The possessive pronoun (used as an adjective) *our* appears four times in the sentences.

Practice 2: Using Intensive Pronouns

1. The coach herself was shocked at her team's performance.
2. I myself scored the game-winning goal.
3. The season itself was otherwise unremarkable.

Practice 3: That *or* Which? Who *or* Whom?

1. that
2. that
3. which
4. who
5. whom
6. Who

22

Verbals

Try to make good language every day,
at the hour best suited to your metabolism.
—FREDERICK BUSCH (1941–2006),
AMERICAN NOVELIST AND STORY WRITER

In this lesson, you'll learn about verbals—gerunds, participles, and infinitives—and their functions in sentences, as outlined in Standards **L.7.1a** and **L.8.1a**.

When is a verb a noun, adjective, or adverb? When it's a verbal!

Reading this riddle and its answer, you may be thinking, *Huh?* But remember this tip from Lesson 19: Many, many words can be used as more than one part of speech. **Verbals** are forms of verbs that do not function as verbs within a sentence. Instead, they function as nouns, adjectives, or adverbs.

There are three types of verbals in English: gerunds, participles, and infinitives. Let's clarify the riddle of verbals by looking at each of these in turn.

Gerunds

Gerunds end with *–ing*. They function as nouns.

A gerund may be the subject of a sentence.

> *Writing improves with practice.*

A gerund may be a predicate nominative.

> *My favorite activity is reading.*

A gerund may be the direct object of a verb or the object of a preposition.

> **Direct object:** *I enjoy walking.*
> **Object of a preposition:** *However, I do not care for running.*

A gerund phrase includes the gerund and any of its modifiers, direct or indirect objects, or other complements (predicate adjective or predicate nominative). Consider the following examples:

> *Eating a variety of colorful fruits and vegetables daily is the foundation of a good diet.*

In this gerund phrase, *a variety of colorful fruits and vegetables* is the direct object of the gerund *eating*, and *daily* is an adverb modifying *eating*.

> *Elena enjoys being a gardener.*

In this gerund phrase, *a gardener* is a predicate nominative that renames the subject, *Elena*, via the gerund *being*.

> *She particularly enjoys getting dirty.*

In this gerund phrase, *dirty* is a predicate adjective describing *she* via the gerund *getting*.

Practice 1: Identifying Gerunds

Underline the gerund phrases in the sentences on the left. Then match each sentence with the description of the function of its gerund on the right.

He actually likes waking before dawn.	Subject
After finishing our meal, we thanked the cook.	Predicate nominative
Our next challenge will be learning the butterfly stroke.	Direct object
Listening to music helps me to concentrate.	Object of a preposition

Participles

Like gerunds, present participles end with *–ing*. Past participles often end with *–ed*, but many have irregular forms, such as *brought*, *done*, and *known*. **Participles** function as adjectives.

> *Swimming, I began to cool off.*
> *The scholar discovered a forgotten story.*

In these sentences, the present participle *swimming* modifies *I*, and the past participle *forgotten* modifies *story*.

Like a gerund phrase, a participial phrase includes the participle and any of its modifiers, direct or indirect objects, or other complements. Consider the following examples:

> *Swimming in the lake that afternoon, I began to cool off.*
> *The scholar discovered a long forgotten story.*

Practice 2: Identifying Participles

Underline the participle or participial phrase in each sentence, and circle the noun it modifies. (One sentence contains a compound participial phrase.)

1. Barking joyfully, the dog greeted us.
2. We'll have to replace these broken parts.
3. Washed and dried thoroughly, the car looked like new.
4. The children laughed on the whirling carousel.

Infinitives

An **infinitive** typically includes the word *to* followed by the simplest form of a verb; for example, *to see* or *to walk*. Infinitives function as nouns, adjectives, and adverbs. Like gerunds and participles, they may form part of a phrase.

In these sentences, the infinitive phrases function as nouns:

> I plan *to leave today*.
> *To change your habits* is *to change your life*.

In these sentences, the infinitive phrases function as adjectives modifying *notebook* and *wish*:

> I need a new notebook *to use as my journal*.
> His wish *to join the varsity soccer team* finally came true.

In these sentences, the infinitive phrases function as adverbs modifying *reviewed* and *am trying*:

> *To study for the test*, I reviewed my notes.
> I am trying *to get better grades*.

You can usually identify an infinitive because it includes the word *to*. Following certain verbs, however, the word *to* may not be used with the infinitive. These verbs include *feel, hear, help, let, make, see,* and *watch*.

> *We could hear him <u>shout</u> from across the roaring river.*
> *Can you please let me <u>take a friend</u>?*
> *She didn't like to dance, but she did like to watch us <u>dance</u>.*

Finally, remember not to confuse an infinitive with a prepositional phrase including the word *to*. In an infinitive, the word *to* is followed by a verb. In a prepositional phrase, the word *to* is followed by a noun.

> *Ronald is going to California to visit his cousin.*

In this sentence, *to visit* is an infinitive. It includes the word *to* followed by the verb visit. *To California* is a prepositional phrase. It includes the word *to* followed by the noun *California*.

Practice 3: Identifying Infinitives

Underline the infinitive phrases in the sentences on the left. Then match each sentence with the description of the function of its infinitive on the right.

To make that soup, we need onion and a butternut squash.	Noun
I would prefer to practice for another hour.	Adjective
My plan to take this shortcut turned into a disaster.	Adverb

Answers

Practice 1: Identifying Gerunds

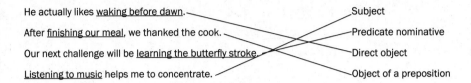

He actually likes <u>waking before dawn</u>. — Subject

After <u>finishing our meal</u>, we thanked the cook. — Predicate nominative

Our next challenge will be <u>learning the butterfly stroke</u>. — Direct object

<u>Listening to music</u> helps me to concentrate. — Object of a preposition

Practice 2: Identifying Participles

1. <u>Barking joyfully</u>, the (dog) greeted us.

2. We'll have to replace these <u>broken</u> (parts).

3. <u>Washed and dried thoroughly</u>, the (car) looked like new.

4. The children laughed on the <u>whirling</u> (carousel).

Practice 3: Identifying Infinitives

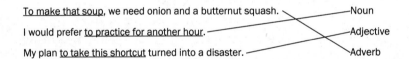

<u>To make that soup</u>, we need onion and a butternut squash. — Noun

I would prefer <u>to practice for another hour</u>. — Adjective

My plan <u>to take this shortcut</u> turned into a disaster. — Adverb

23

Sentence Structure

A well-known writer got collared by a university student who asked, "Do you think I could be a writer?"

"Well," the writer said, "I don't know. . . . Do you like sentences?"

The writer could see the student's amazement. Sentences? Do I like sentences? I am twenty years old and do I like sentences? If he had liked sentences, of course, he could begin, like a joyful painter I knew. I asked him how he came to be a painter. He said, "I liked the smell of paint."

—ANNIE DILLARD (1945–),
AMERICAN ESSAYIST, NOVELIST, AND POET

In this lesson, we'll look at the overall structure of sentences and functions of prepositional phrases and clauses in sentences, as outlined in Standards **L.7.1a** and **L.7.1b**.

Do you like sentences? This question might seem as mysterious to you as it did to the student whom Annie Dillard describes. After all, sentences are everywhere, like the air. They do their job. What is there to like?

You could like the sound of a sentence, based on its rhythm or on how it brings rhyming words together, such as *everywhere* and *air*. You could like variety in sentences: long sentences followed by short sentences, or questions mixed in with declarative sentences. There's plenty to like about sentences, and this enjoyment can begin, if not from pleasure in their sound, with an understanding of their structure.

Prepositional Phrases

A **phrase** is any small group of words. Some phrases act as units within a sentence. These include gerund phrases, participial phrases, and infinitive phrases, which you learned about in the previous lesson.

Another kind of phrase is the **prepositional phrase**. A prepositional phrase includes a preposition and its object. The following are examples of prepositional phrases:

> *during the concert*
> *in their garden*
> *with my friend*

A prepositional phrase may have a compound object.

> *between Earth and the sky*

A prepositional phrase may also include modifiers between the preposition and its object.

> *during the lengthy concert*
> *in their lush, green garden*
> *with my best and oldest friend*
> *between Earth and the clear blue sky*

Additionally, there are a few compound prepositions, such as *according to* and *because of*.

> *according to her*
> *because of them*

Prepositional phrases function as adjectives and adverbs. For example, in these sentences, the prepositional phrases function as adjectives modifying *path*, *home*, and *apartment*:

> The path *through the park* is cracked and crumbling.
> Their home is *in a small apartment* *in the city*.

In these sentences, the prepositional phrases function as adverbs modifying *sit* and *step*:

> Let's sit *in those seats*.
> Step *over the muddy puddle*.

Practice 1: Identifying Prepositional Phrases

Underline the prepositional phrase in each of the sentences below, and identify its function as an adjective or adverb. Circle the word or words it modifies.

1. You can go after dinner.

2. Please park the car in the garage.

3. The sneakers in the closet must be yours.

4. The seagulls flew along the shore.

5. Aren't your keys on the shelf?

Clauses

A **clause** is a group of words that includes a subject and a verb. There are two main types of clauses.

An **independent clause**, or main clause, expresses a complete thought. It can stand alone. The following are independent clauses:

> We ate our breakfast.
> My mother is writing a book.

A **dependent clause**, or subordinate clause, does not express a complete thought. The following are dependent clauses:

> *what she needs most*
> *that I want to see*
> *after she completed her homework*
> *before you leave*

Dependent clauses function as nouns, adjectives, and adverbs. For example, the dependent clause is the subject of the following sentence:

> *What she needs most is a good night's sleep.*

Noun clauses typically begin with such conjunctions as *what, that, which, if, whether, who, whom, when, where, whoever,* and *whatever.*

In the following sentence, the dependent clause functions as an adjective modifying *movie*:

> *The movie that I want to see will be showing this weekend.*

Adjective clauses (or relative clauses) typically begin with one of the relative pronouns, such as *who, whom, which,* or *that.* However, the relative pronoun can sometimes be left out of the sentence, particularly when the relative clause is the object of a verb or preposition.

> *The movie I want to see will be showing this weekend.*

In the following sentences, the dependent clauses function as adverbs modifying *went* and *shut*:

> *After she completed her homework, Susan went for a run.*
> *Please shut the window before you leave.*

Adverbial clauses typically begin with such subordinating conjunctions as *although, because, if, as, when, while, whereas, unless, after, before, until,* and *than.*

Practice 2: Identifying Dependent Clauses

Underline the dependent clause in each of the sentences below, and identify its function as a noun, adjective, or adverb.

1. I tend to fall asleep if I get bored.

2. The girl whom you heard laughing is my sister.

3. I understand that you wish to leave.

4. Unless the weather is terrible, we'll go skating tomorrow.

5. The book that you dropped on the sidewalk is still there.

Sentence Structure

There are four basic types of sentences. Each one is defined by the number and type of clauses it includes.

A **simple sentence** includes just one independent clause, or main clause.

Fido loves to greet visitors.

A simple sentence may include a compound subject or a compound predicate.

Fido and Spot both love to greet visitors.
They bark and leap joyfully.

A **compound sentence** includes two or more main clauses.

Fido loves to greet visitors, and he barks and leaps joyfully.

The clauses in a compound sentence are joined by **coordinating conjunctions**. The coordinating conjunctions are *and, but, for, nor, or, so,* and *yet*.

A **complex sentence** includes one main clause and at least one dependent clause.

Fido barks and leaps joyfully whenever guests arrive.

A **compound-complex sentence** includes two or more main clauses and at least one dependent clause.

Fido loves to greet visitors, so he barks and leaps joyfully whenever guests arrive.

This sentence includes two main clauses: *Fido loves to great visitors* and *he barks and leaps joyfully*. It includes one dependent clause: *whenever guests arrive.*

Practice 3: Identifying Sentence Types

Identify the structure of each sentence below. Underline each independent clause (including any modifiers) once. Underline each dependent clause (including any modifiers) twice.

1. Friendly dogs usually prance around to express their glee, and they also tend to bark a lot.

2. My dog is shy and easily frightened, and she frequently barks when she meets strangers.

3. Timid dogs are often the loudest barkers.

4. Because timid dogs are so often fearful, they can be difficult to train.

5. Life with a happy, well-behaved dog is a good life indeed.

Answers

Practice 1: Identifying Prepositional Phrases

1. Adverb: You (can go) after dinner.

2. Adverb: Please (park) the car in the garage.

3. Adjective: The (sneakers) in the closet must be yours.

4. Adverb: The seagulls (flew) along the shore.

5. Adjective: Aren't your (keys) on the shelf?

Practice 2: Identifying Dependent Clauses

1. Adverb: I tend to fall asleep if I get bored.

2. Adjective: The girl whom you heard laughing is my sister.

3. Noun: I understand that you wish to leave.

4. Adverb: Unless the weather is terrible, we'll go skating tomorrow.

5. Adjective: The book that you dropped on the sidewalk is still there.

Practice 3: Identifying Sentence Types

1. Compound sentence: Friendly dogs usually prance around to express their glee, and they also tend to bark a lot.

2. Compound-complex sentence: My dog is shy and easily frightened, and she frequently barks when she meets strangers.

3. Simple sentence: Timid dogs are often the loudest barkers.

4. Complex sentence: Because timid dogs are so often fearful, they can be difficult to train.

5. Simple sentence: Life with a happy, well-behaved dog is a good life indeed.

24

Commas, Commas, Commas

I was working on the proof of one of my poems all the morning, and took out a comma. In the afternoon I put it back again.
—Oscar Wilde (1854–1900),
Irish playwright, novelist, and poet

In this lesson, you'll learn when and how to use the most widely used punctuation mark: the comma. We'll review many of the various ways that commas are used, including those that are identified in Standards **L.6.2a**, **L.7.2a**, and **L.8.2a**.

In many ways, punctuating your writing is straightforward. For example, don't you end just about all declarative sentences with a period? Don't you end a question with a question mark? And don't you use an exclamation point when you want to show excitement or make a strong point?

Other punctuation marks might seem trickier to you than end punctuation. The comma, for example, might baffle you sometimes. There are a couple of reasons why it might not be clear when to use—and when not to use—a comma. First, the comma is used for many different purposes. The variety of its uses might perplex you. Second, in many instances whether or not to use a comma is up to you. In other words, comma use doesn't always follow hard and fast rules.

Generally, **commas** are used to indicate a pause or break in a sentence. They break up a sentence into chunks that help make meanings clear.

When to Use Commas

1. Use commas in dates.
   May 20, 2018
   Thursday, August 31
   Monday, November 3, 2005

2. Use commas in the greetings and closings of letters.
   Dear John,
   Sincerely yours,
   Hugs and kisses,

3. Use commas in addresses.
   New York, NY
   Washington, DC

4. Use commas to separate items in a series.
   My favorite fruits are apples, oranges, tangerines, and kiwis.

5. Use a comma before the coordinating conjunction in a compound sentence.
   The students got tired of working, but the assignment demanded more time.

   The lessons require some effort, so the students can learn both the rules and their exceptions.

6. Use commas in dialogue or when quoting exact words.
   "Let's go for a walk," Mom suggested.

   "I'm not sure that's a good idea," he responded, "because it looks like it might start to rain soon."

   Ralph Waldo Emerson wrote, "A foolish consistency is the hobgoblin of little minds."

7. Use a comma after an introductory word, phrase, or clause, including the words *yes* and *no*.
    Finally, we arrived home.

    After the long trip, we slept well.

    When we woke the next morning, we enjoyed a lazy breakfast.

    No, we won't be traveling again any time soon.

8. Use commas to set off tag questions or to indicate direct address.
    The sunset is beautiful, isn't it?

    Can you see the new moon, Greta?

    That star, Lawrence, is actually the planet Venus.

9. Use commas to set off **nonrestrictive elements**. These are words, phrases, or clauses that give extra information—that is, information that is not necessary for the overall meaning of a sentence.

    In the following sentence, the title of the song is extra information. It could be left out, and the sentence would still make sense. This means the song title is a nonrestrictive element, so commas are used to set it off.
    Lupita Lopez's latest song, "Mi Corazón, My Heart," is going to be a big hit.

    In the sentence below, however, the title of the song is necessary information. It is *not* a nonrestrictive element, and therefore commas are *not* used.
    Lupita Lopez's song "Mi Corazón, My Heart" is my favorite.

10. Use commas with **coordinate adjectives**. These are adjectives that each modify the same noun equally. You can identify coordinate adjectives because their order can be reversed, and they can be joined with the word *and*.
    Our delicious, colorful meals are also nutritious.

    Our colorful, delicious meals are also nutritious.

    Our colorful and delicious meals are also nutritious.

11. Use commas to indicate a pause or break, especially for the sake of clarity.

   Unclear: *After you study the use of commas will become much clearer.*

   Clear: *After you study, the use of commas will become much clearer.*

. . . .

TIP: When it comes to commas, writers and editors have often been advised, "When in doubt, leave it out!" However, as Bryan A. Garner, author of *Garner's Modern American Usage*, points out, omitting a comma can result in a lack of clarity. Better advice might be, "When in doubt, try it both ways!" Write the sentence both with and without the comma or commas you are unsure about. Read the sentence aloud each way to hear which way seems clearest.

. . . .

Beware of the Comma Splice!

To splice is to join things together. In a **comma splice**, two independent clauses are joined in one sentence by a comma and no coordinating conjunction. Compare these examples:

   I'm tired, I want to go to bed.
   I'm tired, and I want to go to bed.

   Let's read just one more chapter, we can finish the book tomorrow.
   Let's read just one more chapter. We can finish the book tomorrow.

The comma splice in the first example is corrected by adding the coordinating conjunction *and*. The comma splice in the second example is corrected by making each independent clause a separate sentence.

Practice 1: Punctuating a Letter

Correct the punctuation of the letter below. Add or replace end punctuation (periods, question marks, and exclamation points) as needed. Add or remove commas as needed.

11 West 111th Street
New York New York 11111
January 4 2016

Dear Lynne

Do you remember teaching your students, how to use commas. I am having a frustrating though sometimes amusing, experience teaching comma use to my students who find the topic bewildering. I must say I agree don't you.

Their solution to the question of when to insert a comma alas is to sprinkle commas throughout their essays as if they were chocolate sprinkles on an ice cream cone. One student even told me that she has decided to include commas at a rate of one per sentence which looks more professional or so she believes. While I certainly enjoy sprinkles on my ice cream cones I do point out to my students that using commas so liberally is likely to confuse their readers.

Do you have any suggestions for how I can help my students. Any ideas you might have would be much appreciated.

Sincerely
Joy

Practice 2: Using Commas in Sentences

Insert commas where they belong in the following sentences:

1. The Mississippi River the longest in the United States can be said to divide the country into two parts east and west.

2. When you are traveling west from Philadelphia you arrive in Chicago long before you get to Salt Lake City.

3. "Seeing the country by car" added the tour guide "is really the best way to learn what being an American is all about."

4. These days getting to the gate in time for your flight can be difficult because of the requirements that you show your boarding pass and ID take off your shoes and jacket and empty your water bottle to get through security.

5. On the other hand there is no faster easier mode of travel than air flight.

6. Trekking however is actually my favorite way to see the countryside.

7. My family enjoys camping and we try to go on at least one camping trip every year.

8. Yes there are hazards to camping including ants mosquitoes and even bears.

9. Harold that time we saw a bear walking down the trail was terrifying wasn't it?

10. Nevertheless it was an otherwise peaceful relaxing trip.

Answers

Practice 1: Punctuating a Letter

11 West 111th Street
New York, New York 11111
January 4, 2016

Dear Lynne,

Do you remember teaching your students how to use commas? I am having a frustrating, though sometimes amusing, experience teaching comma use to my students, who find the topic bewildering. I must say I agree, don't you?

Their solution to the question of when to insert a comma, alas, is to sprinkle commas throughout their essays as if they were chocolate sprinkles on an ice cream cone. One student even told me that she has decided to include commas at a rate of one per sentence, which looks more professional, or so she believes. While I certainly enjoy sprinkles on my ice cream cones, I do point out to my students that using commas so liberally is likely to confuse their readers.

Do you have any suggestions for how I can help my students? Any ideas you might have would be much appreciated.

Sincerely,
Joy

Practice 2: Using Commas in Sentences

1. The Mississippi River, the longest in the United States, can be said to divide the country into two parts, east and west. (Use commas to set off nonrestrictive elements.)

2. When you are traveling west from Philadelphia, you arrive in Chicago long before you get to Salt Lake City. (Use a comma after an introductory word, phrase, or clause.)

3. "Seeing the country by car," added the tour guide, "is really the best way to learn what being an American is all about." (Use commas in dialogue or when quoting exact words.)

4. These days, getting to the gate in time for your flight can be difficult because of the requirements that you show your boarding pass and ID, take off your shoes and jacket, and empty your water bottle to get through security. (Use a comma after an introductory word, phrase, or clause; use commas to separate items in a series.)

5. On the other hand, there is no faster, easier mode of travel than air flight. (Use a comma after an introductory word, phrase, or clause; use commas with coordinate adjectives.)

6. Trekking, however, is actually my favorite way to see the countryside. (Use commas to set off nonrestrictive elements.)

7. My family enjoys camping, and we try to go on at least one camping trip every year. (Use a comma before the coordinating conjunction in a compound sentence.)

8. Yes, there are hazards to camping, including ants, mosquitoes, and even bears. (Use commas to set off the words *yes* and *no*; use commas to set off nonrestrictive elements; use commas to separate items in a series.)

9. Harold, that time we saw a bear walking down the trail was terrifying, wasn't it? (Use commas to set off tag questions and to indicate direct address.)

10. Nevertheless, it was an otherwise peaceful, relaxing trip. (Use a comma after an introductory word, phrase, or clause; use commas with coordinate adjectives.)

25

Other Punctuation Marks

> *The writer who neglects punctuation or mispunctuates is liable to be misunderstood.*
> —EDGAR ALLAN POE (1809–1849),
> AMERICAN SHORT-STORY WRITER, POET, AND CRITIC

In this lesson, you'll learn when and how to use punctuation marks other than the comma, including those that are mentioned in Standards **L.6.2a**, **L.8.2a**, and **L.8.2b**.

Punctuation marks are rarely the fussy details they might seem to be, given their small size. At the very least, punctuating your sentences correctly shows that you take care with your writing. And at its best, punctuation is an essential aspect of **rhetoric**: the skillful, effective use of language.

The Apostrophe

Apostrophes are those little commas in the air that are so often misused. They have two main uses.

First, they are used in the possessive form of singular and plural nouns.

> *Jane's team spirit.*
> *the boys' team* (The word *boys* already has an *s*, so only an apostrophe is added.)
> *the people's votes* (Like *boys*, the word *people* is plural, but it does not end with an *s*, so an apostrophe and *s* are added.)

Second, they are used to show where letters have been omitted in contractions, as in *I'm* and *won't*.

Although apostrophes are used in the possessive form of nouns, they are *never* used in the possessive pronouns. *Yours, hers, its, ours,* and *theirs* each end with an *s*, so it may be tempting to add an apostrophe. Don't!

Similarly, it is common to confuse possessive pronouns and contractions.

Possessive Pronoun	Contraction
whose (whose friend)	who's (who is)
your (your friend)	you're (you are)
their (their friend)	they're (they are)
its (its head)	it's (it is)

Just remember, possessive pronouns don't have apostrophes!

Quotation Marks

Direct Quotations

Quotation marks are used to show that you are quoting the exact words that someone said, and that you are attributing the words to that person.

> *Jane said, "I want to go to the game with you."*
> *"I will be going," said Marian, "whether or not you go."*

Quotation marks are also used to show that you are quoting the exact words from a text.

> *"Happy families are all alike; every unhappy family is unhappy in its own way," begins Leo Tolstoy's novel* Anna Karenina, *famously.*

TIP: Commas and periods always go inside closing quotation marks.

Words that introduce a quotation (such as *Jane said* in the example above) are set off with a comma. Notice that when the verb (such as *said* and *begins* in the previous examples) follows the quotation, the quotation itself concludes with a comma. However, when the quotation is a question or exclamation, there is no comma, such as in the following examples:

> *"Do you want to come with us?" asked Marian.*
> *"Please don't leave yet!" shouted Jane.*

The end punctuation (question mark or exclamation point) goes inside the quotation marks when the quotation itself is a question or exclamation. However, when the quoted words are part of a larger question or exclamation, the end marks go outside the quotation marks, such as in the following examples:

> *Do I have to listen to Jane saying over and over again, "I want to go"?*

> *I can't believe you said, "It's not a problem"!*

TIP: If you are writing dialogue, indicate changes in speakers by starting a new paragraph for each speaker.

"Why would you want to come with us?" asked Marian, smiling with false sweetness at Jane.

"I think it's not a good idea for you to come," said Steve.

Indirect Quotations

An **indirect quotation** is the restating of something that someone else has said without using his or her exact words. Quotation marks are not used with indirect quotations.

> **Direct quotation:** *Jane said, "I want to go."*
> **Indirect quotation:** *Jane said she wants to go.*

Practice 1: Correcting Punctuation

Rewrite these sentences to correct their errors in punctuation, and briefly describe the error you corrected.

1. I told my parents This is the most important game of the season, so I want to go.
2. Who's parents will be the chaperones at the party after the game? asked my mother.
3. I asked my sister to come, too, but shes not interested in basketball.
4. The crowds screams filled the gymnasium and practically raised it's roof.

Parentheses and Dashes

Like commas (see Lesson 24), **parentheses** and **dashes** are used to set off nonrestrictive elements.

Parentheses give somewhat more emphasis than commas. They are often used to set off dates and citations as well as other nonessential information.

> *William Shakespeare (1564–1616) is often regarded as the greatest dramatist ever to have lived.*

> *In the essay, Ursula LeGuin asks, "Why are Americans afraid of dragons?" (35).*

> *For breakfast this morning, we had scrambled eggs, oranges, and (my favorite) cinnamon toast.*

Dashes lend even more emphasis to nonessential information—more than commas or parentheses do.

> *That morning—the first of the summer—I slept nearly until noon.*

Dashes are also used to set off nonrestrictive elements that are especially long or that include commas.

> *After the cancellation—which was the fourth last-minute cancellation that he had made in as many weeks—I finally realized that he was never going to be a reliable friend.*

> *The three sisters—Sarah, Leah, and Jessica—will be playing in the recital together.*

Practice 2: Using Parentheses and Dashes

Rewrite each sentence with parentheses or dashes where needed.

1. Alfred's greatest fear which that summer haunted his mind with vividly grotesque thoughts every night until he fell asleep was that he would do something terrible while sleepwalking.
2. Eleanor had never heard anything like his story or so she said.
3. On all three days Monday, Tuesday, and Thursday we were lucky enough to catch the early bus from school.
4. But on Friday to our dismay we missed both the early and the late bus and had to walk home.

Ellipses and Dashes

Many different punctuation marks are used to show a pause. End punctuation, such as a period, is used to show the pause at the end of a sentence. Other punctuation marks, such as commas, are used to show pauses within sentences.

Ellipses (. . .) are used to show longer pauses or to show an unfinished thought at the end of a sentence.

We left one snowy afternoon . . . and we never returned.

I'm not sure . . .

A dash gives more emphasis than ellipses do. It can be used to show a more abrupt pause or break or a change in thought.

Please do not mark up those library books—or mine, for that matter.

That's it for today—except I must be forgetting something. Was there something else you needed me to tell you?

In general, use dashes rarely, if at all. If you use too many dashes, your writing will seem choppy or too informal.

Ellipses are also used for another purpose. They are used to show that words have been omitted, or left out, from quoted text.

Read this passage from the Declaration of Independence, and then read the quotation that follows.

> *When in the Course of human events, it becomes necessary for one people to dissolve the political bands which have connected them with another, and to assume among the powers of the earth, the separate and equal station to which the Laws of Nature and of Nature's God entitle them, a decent respect to the opinions of mankind requires that they should declare the causes which impel them to the separation.*

You might quote from this passage as follows:

> *"When in the Course of human events, it becomes necessary for one people to dissolve the political bands which have connected them with another, . . . a decent respect to the opinions of mankind requires that they should declare the causes which impel them to the separation," begins the Declaration of Independence.*

Ellipses appear where words were left out from within a sentence. Include a space before the first ellipsis point and a space after the third ellipsis point. If the omission occurs after the end of a sentence, include a period before the ellipses.

Practice 3: Using Ellipses and Dashes

1. Rewrite this sentence using ellipses in at least one place to show a long pause within the sentence.
   On Saturday we could play games at your house, we could go to the movies, or, I suppose, we could get started on that research project.
2. Rewrite these sentences as one sentence using a dash.
   I'll feel better about the project once we get started. So it's the library for me tomorrow.
3. Write a sentence (or sentence fragment) using ellipses to show an unfinished thought.
4. Using ellipses, as necessary, to show where words have been omitted, revise the following sentence so that the quotation refers only to making no laws abridging freedom of speech or of the press.
   The First Amendment to the Constitution of the United States says, "Congress shall make no law respecting an establishment of religion, or prohibiting the free exercise thereof; or abridging the freedom of speech, or

of the press; or the right of the people peaceably to assemble, and to petition the Government for a redress of grievances."

Answers

Practice 1: Correcting Punctuation

1. I told my parents, "This is the most important game of the season, so I want to go."
   (Use quotation marks with a direct quotation, and set off introductory words with a comma.)

2. "Whose parents will be the chaperones at the party after the game?" asked my mother. (Use the possessive pronoun *whose*, not a contraction; use quotation marks with a direct quotation; and include the question mark within the quotation marks.)

3. I asked my sister to come, too, but she's not interested in basketball.
   (Use an apostrophe with the contraction *she's*.)

4. The crowd's screams filled the gymnasium and practically raised its roof.
   (Use an apostrophe with the possessive noun *crowds*, and use the possessive pronoun *its*, not a contraction.)

Practice 2: Using Parentheses and Dashes

Rewrite each sentence with parentheses or dashes where needed.

1. Alfred's greatest fear—which that summer haunted his mind with vividly grotesque thoughts every night until he fell asleep—was that he would do something terrible while sleepwalking.

2. Eleanor had never heard anything like his story (or so she said).
   or
   Eleanor had never heard anything like his story—or so she said.

3. On all three days—Monday, Tuesday, and Thursday—we were lucky enough to catch the early bus from school.

4. But on Friday (to our dismay) we missed both the early and the late bus and had to walk home.
   or
   But on Friday—to our dismay—we missed both the early and the late bus and had to walk home.

Practice 3: Using Ellipses and Dashes

1. On Saturday we could play games at your house, we could go to the movies . . . or, I suppose, we could get started on that research project.
2. I'll feel better about the project once we get started—so it's the library for me tomorrow.
3. *Sample response:* I suppose that our other plans can wait until . . .
4. The First Amendment to the Constitution of the United States says, "Congress shall make no law . . . abridging the freedom of speech, or of the press."

Section 6

Finishing and Publishing Your Writing

At the end of the writing process, you review your composition and make sure that every detail is just as you want it. This stage of the writing process is often the most pleasurable. You can enjoy the fruit of your efforts as you polish it to share it with others.

As a young writer, you've likely never thought of sharing your writing by publishing it. Doesn't publishing seem like something only adult, professional writers do? Well, think again. Writing by children and teens is published in many places—from school bulletin boards to newspapers, magazines (both print and online), and books. The last lesson of this book gives you ideas about how to find a place that might publish *your* writing. Wouldn't you like to see your name in print as the author of a well-written essay, poem, or story?

26

Proofreading Your Writing

*Sometimes I think my writing sounds like I walked
out of the room and left the typewriter running.*
—GENE FOWLER (1890–1960),
AMERICAN JOURNALIST AND SCREENWRITER

You're in the home stretch! In this lesson, you'll learn some tips for proofreading your writing. Using strategies to improve expression in conventional language is the focus of Standard **L.6.1e**, and spelling correctly (one of the main purposes of proofreading) is the focus of Standards **L.6.2b**, **L.7.2b**, and **L.8.2c**.

Note: As you *read this lesson, keep an eye out for anything that seems a little bit . . . off. Put a mark next to or circle words or punctuation that give you pause—they're sure to come up later.*

Proofreading is the final stage of the writing process. During this stage, you take one last, close look at your composition so that you can find and correct any misspellings, misteaks in punctuation, and other small errors. These errors might not seem like a big deal, but they can cause problems. They can distract or even confuse your readers. They can also make it seem as though your words and ideas are not to be taken seriously.

How to Proofread

Proofreading can be especially challenging, after you have given a lot of your time to a piece of writing. You've already looked at it so many times that it can be hard to see any errors! How can you sharpen your vision? Here are a few tips:

- **Take a break!** Don't try to proofread your writing immediately after you finish editing it. Put it away for at least an hour or two and return to it with a fresh perspective.

- **Work without distraction.** Proofreading well requires focus. Don't try to proofread with loud music blaring or in front of the TV.

- **Print out your composition.** If you've been looking at your writing on the screen, printing it out is one way to get a fresh look at it. Changing the font, including its size, can also help you see what you mght otherwise miss.

- **Read your composition out loud or backward.** These methods of reading force you to look closely at every word.

- **Make a checklist of your common errors.** Do you often use sentence fragments or comma splices? Are there particular words that you frequently misspell? Keep a list of your common errors so that you remember to look for them while you proofread.

- **When in doubt, look it up.** Use your dictionary and a grammar handbook to help you out when you're not sure if something that looks like an error really is an error.

- **Remember, as with everything, the more you do it, the better you'll get.** Over time, you may find that you develop a systematic appraoch to proofreading. You'll miss fewer errors even as you become more efficient.

Common Spelling Errors

One major purpose of proofreading is to catch spelling errors. However, there are so many errors to be made, because there are so many exceptions to them, rules such as writing *i* before *e* except after *c* are of limited use. Fortunately, there are a few general principals you can follow to help you avoid—or catch—errors.

- **Watch out for letters that have been transposed, or appear in reverse order.** For example, *traet* could easily be mistaken for *treat*.

- **Watch out for missing letters.** How easily you could overlook the *i* that is missing from *mssing*!

- **Pay attention to words with prefixes. Prefixes** are word parts added to the beginnings of words.
  - When a prefix (such as *mis–*) is added to a word (such as *spell*), do not drop or double letters in the base word; for example: *misspell*.
  - Note, however, that some prefixes themselves have variable spellings. The prefix *in–* (as in *inexpensive*), for example, can also appear as *im–* (as in *impossible*) or even *il–* (as in *illegal*).

- **Pay attention to words with suffixes. Suffixes** are word parts added to the endings of words.
  - In general, drop a final silent *e* when adding a suffix that begins with a vowel. For example, *love* becomes *loving*. Keep the final silent *e* when adding a suffix that begins with a consonant. For example, *love* becomes *lovely*. If the silent *e* comes after a vowel, however, drop it when adding any suffix. For example, *argue* becomes *arguing* and *argument*.
  - In general, if a word ends with *y* preceded by a consonant, change the *y* to an *i* when adding any suffix but *–ing*. For example, *worry* becomes *worried* and *worrying*.

- In general, if a word ends in a single consonant preceded by a vowel and the word has one syllable or ends on a stress, double the final consonant when adding a suffix. For example, *win* becomes *winning*, and *forget* becomes *forgetting*.

- **Pay attention to plurals.** Add *–s* to form the plural of most words. In general, add *–es* in the following cases:
  - If a noun ends with *y* preceded by a consonant, change the *y* to an *i* and add *–es*. For example, *baby* becomes *babies*, but *toy* becomes *toys*.
  - If a noun ends with *o* preceded by a consonant, add *–es*. For example, *potato* becomes *potatoes*, but *video* becomes *videos*.
  - If a noun ends with *s*, *ss*, *sh*, *ch*, *x*, or *z*, add *–es*. For example, *kiss* becomes *kisses*, and *witch* becomes *witches*.

- **Watch out for commonly confused words.** We'll take a look at some of these in Lesson 28.

And also remember to keep a list of words you often misspell on your checklist of common errors Additionally, when it comes to checking and correcting your spelling, there's nothing heroic about doing it all on your own. If necessary, use a dictionary to help you out. If you often find it difficult to find correct spellings in the dictionary, try using a misspeller's dictionary.

But What About Spell-Checking and Grammar-Checking Programs?

Spell-checking and grammar-checking programs like the ones that may be included with your word processing software can be helpful aids, but you cannot rely on them entirely. A spell-checking program will not identify every misspelling.

For example, the spell-checking tool of a popular word processing program finds no problem with the following sentence:

> *This essay is grate!*

Grate is the correct spelling for a couple of words: a noun meaning "a frame of metal bars that serves as a cover or guard" and a verb meaning "to irritate." Neither of these is the word needed in this sentence which is the adjective meaning "very good, excellent." This adjective is spelled *great*.

Similarly the grammar-checking tool of the same popular word processing program finds no problem with the following sentence:

> *This step may be the last but it far from the least.*

Notice that the second clause of this sentence is missing a verb and that there should be a comma before the coordinating conjunction *but*.

Not only are these programs likely to miss errors, but they may also confuse you by saying that there is an error where there isn't actually any problem. For example, spell-checking programs may fail to recognize certain less common but correctly spelled words such as *freewriting* and *verbals* (both of which, of course, we've used throughout this book). And they may not recognize many proper nouns. For example, a program is likely to recognize the common name *Thomas* but may not recognize its less common variant *Thomasina*.

· ·

TIP: Do not rely on spell-checking and grammar-checking programs to do your proofreading for you. Check any words, phrases, and sentences that they call out as needing attention, and then review your writing for errors yourself.

· ·

The Final Step: Formatting

If your writing for an assignment, review the assignment one last time to check for information on how to format your essay or narrative (or recall your teacher's usual instructions). If you are using a word processor, be sure that you've set the margins correctly, spaced the lines properly (double-spaced or single-spaced?), and made the breaks between paragraphs clear. If you are writing by hand, be sure that you have left time to write out a clean final copy, with no words left out, cross-outs, or smudges. An essay that looks neat is bound to make a good first impression.

Practice 1: Proofreading Practice

This lesson includes 10 errors: five spelling errors and five punctuation errors, including a comma splice. Did you notice them? Identify and correct them.

Practice 1: Proofreading Practice

Spelling Error #1:
Page 192: *mistakes* is misspelled as misteaks

Spelling Error #2:
Page 192: *might* is misspelled as mght

Spelling Error #3:
Page 193: *approach* is misspelled as appraoch

Spelling Error #4:
Page 193: *principles* is misspelled as principals

Spelling Error #5:
Page 195: *you're* is misspelled as your

Punctuation Error #1:
Page 192:
This sentence does not need a comma:
Proofreading can be especially challenging, after you have given a lot of your time to a piece of writing.

Rewrite as:
Proofreading can be especially challenging after you have given a lot of your time to a piece of writing.

Punctuation Error #2:
Page 193:
This sentence has a comma splice:
However, there are so many errors to be made, because there are so many exceptions to them, rules such as writing i *before* e *except after* c *are of limited use.*

Rewrite as:

However, there are so many errors to be made because there are so many exceptions to them—rules such as writing i *before* e *except after* c *are of limited use.*

Punctuation Error #3:

Page 194:

Insert a period at the end of this sentence:

And also remember to keep a list of words you often misspell on your checklist of common errors.

Punctuation Error #4:

Page 195:

A comma should precede *which* here:

Neither of these is the word needed in this sentence, which is the adjective meaning "very good, excellent."

Punctuation Error #5:

Page 195:

A comma should follow *Similarly* here:

Similarly, the grammar-checking tool of the same popular word processing program finds no problem with the following sentence:

_____

_____

27

Avoiding Common Errors, Part 1

Life is tons of discipline. Your first discipline is your vocabulary,
then your grammar and your punctuation.
—ROBERT FROST (1874–1963),
AMERICAN POET

This lesson and the next give an overview of common errors. These are the kinds of errors you might catch—and must correct!—while proofreading. Using strategies to improve expression in conventional language is the focus of Standard **L.6.1e**, problems with pronouns are the focus of Standards **L.6.1c** and **L.6.1d**, and problems with voice and mood are the focus of Standard **L.8.1d**.

One good thing about common errors is that because they're common, you know to watch out for them. Among the errors to watch out for are errors of agreement and other problems in which elements of a sentence that should be consistent are not. We'll look at these kinds of errors in this lesson.

Common Error 1: Problems with Subject/Verb Agreement

Every verb and its subject must agree in number. In other words, a singular subject goes with a singular verb; a plural subject goes with a plural verb.

> **Singular:** The girl laughs.
> **Plural:** The girls laugh.

Easy enough, right? However, problems with subject/verb agreement can occur for any number of reasons. Errors like this can creep into your writing during the revision process; for example, you might change one part of a sentence without checking that you've maintained subject/verb agreement. Errors can also occur when it's not immediately clear whether a subject is singular or plural.

- Sometimes, a compound subject expresses a single idea and can take a singular verb.
  War and peace is a common subject for debate in political circles.
  Love and marriage is the theme of many movies.

- If a compound subject is joined by *or* or *nor*, the verb agrees in number with the closest noun.
  Singular verb for singular *cat*: *Either a dog or a cat <u>makes</u> a good pet.*
  Plural verb for plural *plants*: *Either a pet or plants <u>make</u> good hobbies.*

Practice 1: Subject/Verb Agreement

Choose the verb that best completes each of the following sentences.

1. Singers and dancers (make, makes) the stage show more exciting and colorful.
2. The contestants for a place in the show (is, are) waiting in the lobby of the theatre.
3. Would-be performers often (take, takes) years to realize that they have no talent.

4. The costumes for the show (doesn't, don't) convey accurate information about the historical period.

5. Either a pink leotard or black tap shoes (is, are) required for a part in the show.

Common Error 2: Problems with Pronoun Agreement

Remember (from Lesson 21) that the antecedent of a pronoun is the word or phrase that the pronoun replaces or refers to. A pronoun and its antecedent must agree in number and in person.

Agreeing in Number

Singular pronouns agree with singular antecedents, and plural pronouns agree with plural antecedents. For example:

> **Singular pronouns for a singular antecedent:** *Sammy wanted to play kickball, so he asked his big brother to go with him to the playground.*

> **Plural pronoun for a plural antecedent:** *The birds flew away, because they saw the cat coming.*

There are a couple of instances in which trouble can occur. For example, remember that a compound antecedent is plural. In the following sentence, the plural pronoun *they* refers to both *sweater* and *coat* together:

> *Wear a sweater underneath your coat, and together they will keep you warm.*

The indefinite pronouns can also cause trouble. These pronouns are singular: *anybody, anyone, anything, everybody, everyone, everything, somebody, someone, something, another, each, either, neither, nobody, nothing, none,* and *one.* Compare the following examples:

> **Correct:** *Everyone must go back to his or her seat!*

> **Incorrect:** *Everyone must go back to their seat!*

The repetition of "his or her" can become awkward. To some, it is acceptable to use *their* as a gender-neutral singular pronoun (as in the sentence labeled "Incorrect" above). Another option is to rewrite the sentence to avoid the need for a singular pronoun. For example:

> *All the children must go back to their seats!*

Agreeing in Person

First-person pronouns (*I, we, me, us*) agree with first-person antecedents, second-person pronouns (*you*) agree with second-person antecedents, and third-person pronouns (*he, she, it, they*) agree with third-person antecedents. Compare the following examples:

> **Correct:** *If a child lives in a home with many books, he or she is likely to come to enjoy reading.*
> **Incorrect:** *If a child lives in a home with many books, you are likely to come to enjoy reading.*

Abruptly switching from the third person (*child*) to the second person (*you*) is likely to confuse readers. The third-person pronouns (*he or she*) should be used.

Vague Pronouns

Be sure that each pronoun has a clear antecedent. In particular, watch out for pronouns with more than one possible antecedent. Consider the following example:

> *When Thomas came to visit Josiah, he was overjoyed.*

Who was overjoyed—Thomas or Josiah? Rewrite the sentence to clarify.

> **Either:** *When he went to visit Josiah, Thomas was overjoyed.*
> **Or:** *When Thomas came to visit him, Josiah was overjoyed.*

Also watch out for references to an undefined "they," as in the following example:

> *It's impossible not to break the rules, because they just make too many of them.*

Who are "they"? Use an exact noun (or nouns) to clarify.

It's impossible not to break the rules, because principals and teachers just make too many of them.

Practice 2: Pronoun Agreement

Rewrite each sentence, correcting or clarifying its pronoun usage.

1. Miriam met her mother at the store, and she took care of the shopping much more quickly together.

2. Somebody parked their car in front of our driveway.

3. If a student keeps arriving late to school, the principal will ask to speak to you.

4. Before Mizuki spoke with her mother on the phone, she was worried. (*Rewrite to show that it was Mizuki who was worried.*)

5. Before Mizuki spoke with her mother on the phone, she was worried. (*Now rewrite to show that it was Mizuki's mother who was worried.*)

6. There's litter everywhere! They really don't care about the school.

Common Error 3: Shifts in Voice and Mood

As you probably already know, consistency in verb tense, number, and person is necessary for clarity. Consistency in verb voice and mood is also needed for clarity.

In general, do not start a sentence in the active voice and shift to the passive voice.

> *Nick baked a big batch of chocolate-chip cookies, and he was thanked many times for sharing them with his friends.*

Correct this sentence by maintaining the active voice throughout.

> *Nick baked a big batch of chocolate-chip cookies, and his friends thanked him many times for sharing the cookies with them.*

Similarly, do not shift from mood to mood for no reason. For example, in the following sentences, the mood shifts from the indicative to the imperative:

> *The recipe has only four steps. First, cut up the bread.*

Correct these sentences by maintaining the indicative mood throughout.

> *The recipe has only four steps. The first is to cut up the bread.*

Consider the following example, in which the mood shifts from the subjunctive to the indicative:

> *If Dad were home, he will make spaghetti for dinner.*

For consistency, this sentence should conclude in the conditional mood.

> *If Dad were home, he would make spaghetti for dinner.*

Practice 3: Shifts in Voice and Mood

Rewrite each sentence, correcting any shifts in voice or mood.

1. The children thought the cartoon was hilarious, but it was loathed by their parents.

2. It's going to take a while for us to get there. First, walk to the bus stop.

3. If you came to the park, we will play soccer together.

Answers

Practice 1: Subject/Verb Agreement
1. make
2. are
3. take
4. don't
5. are

Practice 2: Pronoun Agreement
1. Miriam met her mother at the store, and they took care of the shopping much more quickly together.
2. Somebody parked his or her car in front of our driveway.
3. If a student keeps arriving late to school, the principal will ask to speak to him or her.
4. Before she spoke with her mother on the phone, Mizuki was worried.
5. Before Mizuki spoke with her on the phone, her mother was worried.
6. There's litter everywhere! So many of the students here really don't care about the school.

Practice 3: Shifts in Voice and Mood
1. The children thought the cartoon was hilarious, but their parents loathed it.
2. It's going to take a while for us to get there. First, we need to walk to the bus stop.
3. If you came to the park, we would play soccer together.

28

Avoiding Common Errors, Part 2

The difference between the almost right word and the right word is the difference between the lightning bug and the lightning.
—Mark Twain (1835–1910), American novelist and humorist

This lesson offers an overview of a few more common errors. Using strategies to improve expression in conventional language is the focus of Standard **L.6.1e**, misplaced and dangling modifiers are the focus of Standard **L.7.1c**, and spelling correctly is the focus of Standards **L.6.2b**, **L.7.2b**, and **L.8.2c**.

In this lesson we'll look at a few common problems with sentence structure and then conclude by reviewing some commonly confused words. After you complete this lesson, go back to review both this lesson and the previous one. Which of the errors reviewed in these lessons are *your* common errors?

Common Error 4: The Comma Splice and Other Run-On Sentences

The comma splice is so common that we've already looked at it, in Lesson 24. In a comma splice, two independent clauses are joined in one sentence by a comma and no coordinating adjective. Compare these examples:

> *I'm already weary of the cold, now a blizzard is coming.*
> *I'm already weary of the cold, and now a blizzard is coming.*

> *We can try to enjoy the storm, we can make popcorn and watch movies.*
> *We can try to enjoy the storm. We can make popcorn and watch movies.*

The comma splice in the first example is corrected by adding the coordinating conjunction *and*. The comma splice in the second example is corrected by making each independent clause a separate sentence.

A **run-on sentence** is similar to a comma splice. (In fact, some grammarians see the comma splice as a type of run-on sentence.) In a run-on sentence, two independent clauses are joined in one sentence without a comma or coordinating adjective. It can be corrected in the same ways as a comma splice. See these examples:

> *I'm worried I don't have boots that fit.*
> *I'm worried because I don't have boots that fit.*
> *I'm worried. I don't have boots that fit.*

Notice that in the second example, the run-on was corrected by changing the independent clause I don't have boots that fit to a dependent clause: because I don't have boots that fit.

Practice 1: Correcting Comma Splices and Run-Ons

Rewrite each sentence, correcting any comma splice errors.

1. Students once used typewriters for their assignments, personal computers were not yet common.

2. Typewriters are now uncommon, it can be hard to find the ribbons needed to use one.

3. Many students have computers at home anyway they still type with just two fingers.

4. Ms. Katz tells us not to rely on the spell-check feature on our computers, she wants us to learn to proofread instead.

Common Error 5: The Incomplete Sentence

A **complete sentence** includes both a subject and a predicate and can stand alone. The **subject** is the noun or noun phrase that the sentence tells about. The **predicate** is the part of the sentence that includes the verb and its modifiers. An incomplete sentence, or **sentence fragment**, lacks a subject or predicate or is a dependent clause punctuated like a complete sentence. Compare these examples:

> *Let's go to the beach this afternoon. Because I'm so tired of this heat.*
> *Let's go to the beach this afternoon because I'm so tired of this heat.*
> *Let's go to the beach this afternoon. I'm so tired of this heat.*

In the first example, the dependent clause *Because I'm so tired of this heat* is punctuated like a complete sentence. This fragment is corrected in the second example by joining the independent and dependent clause in one sentence. It is corrected in the third example by changing the dependent clause to an independent clause, *I'm so tired of this heat.*

Practice 2: Identifying and Correcting Incomplete Sentences

Identify each incomplete sentence and rewrite it as a complete sentence.

1. Writing can be difficult.

2. Although I am trying to improve.

3. Talking is not so different from writing.

4. Using big words to impress the reader.

Common Error 6: Misplaced and Dangling Modifiers

A **misplaced modifier** is a modifier (adjective, adverb, or modifying phrase or clause) that does not appear near the word it modifies. Confusion can result! Consider the following examples:

We had hot bowls of cereal for breakfast.
I gave the books to him with the tattered covers.
It was hot, so we ate the ice cream we had bought quickly.

These sentences would be much clearer if the modifying phrases were placed nearer to the words they modify. For example:

We had bowls of hot cereal for breakfast.
I gave the books with the tattered covers to him.
It was hot, so we quickly ate the ice cream we had bought.

A **dangling modifier** results when its subject is not named anywhere in the sentence. Consider the following sentence:

Walking out the door this morning, the pigeons were quarreling on the lawn.

This sentence seems to be saying that the pigeons walked out the door. However, it is the (unnamed) speaker who walked out the door.

There are a few ways to fix this sentence. One way is to revise the main clause of the sentence so that it names the person (*I*) who did the action in the modifying phrase (*walked*).

Walking out the door this morning, I saw the pigeons quarreling on the lawn.

Another way to fix this sentence is to change the modifying phrase into a clause that names the person (*I*) who did the action (*walked*).

When I walked out the door this morning, the pigeons were quarreling on the lawn.

Practice 3: Misplaced and Dangling Modifiers

Rewrite each sentence, correcting any misplaced or dangling modifiers.

1. We saw a dog running in their yard with wild fur.

2. To overcome your stage fright, practicing in front of other people could help.

3. Swimming in the lake, thunder rumbled in the distance, so I got out of the water and found shelter.

4. Having failed to get a part in the play, it suddenly became very important to me to join the track team instead.

Common Error 7: Commonly Confused Words

Many errors are the result of writing a similar, correctly spelled word in place of the word that belongs in a sentence. These are the kinds of misspellings that a spell-check program is unlikely to catch. Here are 10 examples of commonly confused words:

accept and *except*

Accept is a verb meaning "to receive" or "to agree." *Except* is a preposition or conjunction meaning "other than."

> *The teacher <u>accepted</u> most of Kaeley's excuse, <u>except</u> for the part about how the dog ate her homework.*

advice and *advise*

Advise is a verb meaning "to give an opinion or recommendation." In other words, it is the verb that expresses the action of giving advice. *Advice* is a noun meaning "recommendation."

> *The teacher <u>advised</u> the students to take her <u>advice</u> and study hard for the examination.*

affect and *effect*

Affect is usually used as a verb meaning "to influence." *Effect* is usually used as a noun meaning "result."

> *The <u>effect</u> of good study habits is good grades, and these in turn can <u>affect</u> the availability of later opportunities.*

already and *all ready*

Already means "by this time." *All ready* means "prepared."

> *By the time I started my homework, my friend Amy had <u>already</u> finished hers. I didn't have much to do, so I expected to be <u>all ready</u> for school well before my bedtime.*

bad and *badly*

Bad is an adjective, and *badly* is an adverb.

> *The teacher feels <u>bad</u> when any of his students perform <u>badly</u> on a test.*

like and *as*

Like is traditionally used as a preposition and therefore should be used to introduce a noun or noun phrase. *As* can be used as a conjunction and can be used to introduce a verb or clause.

> **Incorrect:** *The sequel ended just <u>like</u> the earlier movie did.*
> **Correct:** *The sequel ended just <u>as</u> the earlier movie did.*
> **Correct:** *The sequel's ending was just <u>like</u> the earlier movie's.*

loose and *lose*

Loose is an adjective meaning "free" or "not tight." *Lose* is a verb meaning "to come to be without [something]."

> *The straps on your backpack are too <u>loose</u>. You might <u>lose</u> your homework on the way to school.*

maybe and *may be*

Both of these are used to refer to a possibility, but they are different parts of speech. *Maybe* is an adverb. *May be* is a verb.

> **Either:** <u>Maybe</u> we will have a quiz tomorrow.
> **Or:** The quiz <u>may be</u> tomorrow.

principal and *principle*

Both of these words are used as nouns. A *principle* is a rule or policy. A principal is a leader, particularly the head of a school. *Principal* is also an adjective meaning "highest in rank or importance."

> The <u>principal</u> of our school insists that we observe the <u>principle</u> of fair play in all of our competitions.
>
> One of the <u>principal</u> reasons to write well is so that you can communicate your ideas effectively.

than and *then*

Than is a conjunction used in comparisons. *Then* is an adverb used to show sequence.

> I will work on this essay until it's much better <u>than</u> the last one I wrote, and <u>then</u> I might try to get it published.

Practice 4: Commonly Confused Words

Choose the word that best completes each of the following sentences.

1. I'm having a hard time (*accepting, excepting*) all the changes you've made to the rules.

2. Could you please (*advice, advise*) me regarding which class would be most suitable for me?

3. She was surprised to find that one of the (*affects, effects*) of running more often was that she had more energy.

4. I want us to be (*already, all ready*) to go in 10 minutes.

5. The other kids in the neighborhood all felt (*bad*, *badly*) when we lost our pet snake.

6. Please, do (*like*, *as*) I say!

7. If you aren't more careful, you'll (*loose*, *lose*) that earring!

8. It (*maybe*, *may be*) that we agreed to do too much.

9. If you don't feel well, the (*principal*, *principle*) thing to do is get more rest.

10. I think that Gregory got the role not because he is more talented, but because he wants it far more (*than*, *then*) anyone else.

Answers
Practice 1: Correcting Comma Splices and Run-Ons

1. *Sample response:* Students once used typewriters for their assignments, because personal computers were not yet common.
2. *Sample response:* Because typewriters are now uncommon, it can be hard to find the ribbons needed to use one.
3. *Sample response:* Although many students have computers at home, they still type with just two fingers anyway.
4. *Sample response:* Ms. Katz tells us not to rely on the spell-check feature on our computers. She wants us to learn to proofread instead.

Practice 2: Identifying and Correcting Incomplete Sentences

2. *Sample response:* I am trying to improve.
4. *Sample response:* Using big words to impress the reader isn't a good idea.

Practice 3: Misplaced and Dangling Modifiers

1. *Sample response:* We saw a dog with wild fur running in their yard.
2. *Sample response:* Practicing in front of other people could help you overcome your stage fright.
3. *Sample response:* Swimming in the lake, I heard thunder rumble in the distance, so I got out of the water and found shelter.
4. *Sample response:* After I failed to get a part in the play, it suddenly became very important to me to join the track team instead.

Practice 4: Commonly Confused Words

1. accepting
2. advise
3. effects
4. all ready
5. bad
6. as
7. lose
8. may be
9. principal
10. than

29

A Final Review

I'm not a very good writer, but I'm an excellent rewriter.
—JAMES A. MICHENER (1907–1997),
AMERICAN NOVELIST AND SHORT-STORY WRITER

Congratulations! You've made it just about to the end of this book. In this lesson you'll have an opportunity to review what you've learned and gain insight on your own writing process.

As you may have come to understand by working through the lessons in this book, a commitment to writing well requires a commitment to the writing process. This understanding may bring relief. Although the process of prewriting, drafting, revising, editing, and proofreading a piece of writing might take longer than other approaches you've taken, it takes the pressure off. You don't have to get it right the first time; instead, you can get it right bit by bit.

This final lesson provides a list of insights from throughout the book. Review this list and then do the final practice activity to make these tips your own.

TIP 1: The single best way to improve your writing . . .

One of the most effective ways to improve your writing doesn't involve writing at all. The secret: Read! If you read just a bit every day, you'll learn how to engage readers, help readers understand your ideas, and use language in fresh and exciting ways—as if by magic! Your writing will almost certainly improve.

TIP 2: Define your purpose and keep it in mind.

Your purpose is your reason for writing. Even if you are writing for a school assignment, define your own specific purpose for writing. If you do so, you can make the assignment your own—and make your writing stand out.

TIP 3: Match your tone to your audience and purpose.

The tone is the quality of the your (or your narrator's) voice, and your audience is the people whom you expect to read your writing. In general, use a formal tone for serious audiences and purposes. If your audience or purpose is more familiar or casual, then it is entirely appropriate to use a familiar, casual tone.

TIP 4: Take the pressure off yourself!

Use the writing process! Each stage of this process gives you another opportunity to generate and further refine your ideas and language. Therefore, you don't have to get it right (whatever "right" might be) the first time, nor even the second, third, or fourth time.

TIP 5: Keep the *storm* in *brainstorm* in mind.

Storms are chaotic and leave messes behind. So don't hold back or worry about how strange or messy your writing might get while you're brainstorming (or freewriting or making an idea web). Once you've made your ideas concrete by writing them down, it'll be that much easier to organize and make sense out of them later.

TIP 6: Your thesis should answer the question *So what?*

A strong thesis statement does more than just clearly state the topic and your point of view. It also indicates why your topic matters to you and your readers.

TIP 7: Even a rough outline is better than none.

Writing an outline might seem like extra work, but it's work well done. It can reveal whether your thesis is usable or weak, and it can reveal gaps or areas of weakness in the development or support of your central idea or ideas. Most important, it provides a path for you to follow once you are immersed in the drafting process.

TIP 8: Organize carefully!

The organizational pattern (or patterns) you apply in a piece of writing helps you emphasize certain relationships among the ideas, events, and details in the composition. Additionally, the organizational pattern helps you guide your reader through your essay or narrative, so that he or she is more likely to finish reading with a good understanding of what you hoped to convey.

TIP 9: Make time to plan, even when time is limited.

When you have only a short time to complete a response to a prompt, it might seem that you have no time to do anything but write. But however limited your time may be, it's best to use some of that time to make a plan, even just a rough plan. The result will likely be better organized and developed than anything you could write off the top of your head.

TIP 10: Grab your reader's attention.

Make sure that your opening will grab your reader's attention and engage him or her with your topic and point of view. Here are some options:

- Begin with a shocking statement.

- Ask an engaging question.

- Begin with a compelling quotation, particularly from an authority on your subject.

- Describe an imaginary scenario or actual character or scene.

- In a narrative, try beginning in medias res ("in the middle of things").

- Give one or more examples or share an anecdote that illustrates your thesis.

- Adapt a familiar quotation to your own purposes.

TIP 11: Put off writing the introduction.

If you're having trouble drafting an introduction, remember that you can always skip it and begin by writing the body paragraphs. After you have sense of how your ideas are developing, you can go back to the beginning and draft a first paragraph. You'll want your final draft to be in order, of course, but you don't actually have to *write* it in order.

TIP 12: Figure out what strategies help you avoid writer's block.

There are several ways to break through if you find that you're completely blocked.

- Try freewriting on your topic.

- Talk to a parent, a friend, or another trusted person about what you are hoping to say.

- Read a published article or story in a form similar to the form you are writing, to absorb its structure, strategies, and use of language.

- Go back and reread the assignment; you may be missing a big clue.

- Give it a rest, overnight if possible, and then come back to your work with fresh eyes the next day.

TIP 13: In an argument, use the best evidence.

The best evidence is evidence that your audience will find convincing. Remember this idea as you think about what evidence to include. Will your audience be more convinced by a personal anecdote or by data from a survey? What kinds of quotations will your audience find most convincing?

TIP 14: In a narrative, use narrative techniques.

A narrative technique is a method used to tell a story, such as description and dialogue. Use narrative techniques to show what happened instead of summarizing what happened. Bring the experience to life for your readers.

TIP 15: Leave enough time for revising, editing, and proofreading.

There's no need to worry about making mistakes in the earlier stages of the writing process as long as you give yourself enough time for the later stages of the process.

- During the revising stage, you focus on the big picture: the development and organization of your ideas.

- During the editing stage, you consider the tone of your composition, as well as sentence structure and your choice of words.

- During the proofreading stage, you attend to the details: language use, spelling, and punctuation.

TIP 16: Take a break before you start to revise.

Remember, *revise* means "to see again." Therefore, before you start revising a draft, give yourself some time to get a fresh perspective on it.

TIP 17: Avoid bad writing habits—or edit to fix them.

The more you write, the greater ease you'll have using language overall and the more likely you'll be to follow good writing habits naturally. But whenever poor wording does creep in, you can fix it during the editing process. Try to avoid:

- wordiness.

- clichés and slang.

- using a thesaurus to find impressive words.

- vague language.

TIP 18: Adopt good writing habits as you draft, revise, and edit.

- When appropriate, use domain-specific vocabulary.

- Use transitions to show the relationships between ideas and events.

- Vary your sentence structure.

- When appropriate, use text features to organize information.

TIP 19: Use these proofreading strategies to sharpen your vision.

- Take a break.

- Work without distraction.

- Print out your composition.

- Read your composition out loud or backward.

- Make a checklist of your common errors.

- When in doubt, look it up in the dictionary or a grammar handbook.

TIP 20: Watch out for the following common errors.

Add these errors to your personal checklist of errors to look out for—along with the errors that are common for *you*.

- problems with subject/verb agreement

- problems with pronoun agreement or with vague pronouns

- shifts in voice and mood

- comma splices and other run-on sentences

- sentence fragments

- misplaced and dangling modifiers

- mistaking commonly confused words

Practice 1: Reviewing the Final Review

Given a list to read, people often skim through it. Did you skim through the list above? Now take the time to read it again, more slowly. Highlight or circle any of the tips that you find especially helpful or that address areas of writing that are especially troublesome for you.

Next, review the table of contents and identify the lessons that address your problem areas. Review those lessons—or, better yet, dog-ear them for later review, when you're working on your next writing assignment for school.

After you've completed this review, go on to the next lesson, which shares tips for publishing your writing. Are you ready?

30

Seeing Your Work Out in the World

You must keep sending work out; you must never let a manuscript do nothing but eat its head off in a drawer. You send that work out again and again, while you're working on another one. If you have talent, you will receive some measure of success—but only if you persist.
—Isaac Asimov (1920–1992) American novelist and essayist

Have you ever thought of publishing your writing? Perhaps not, but this lesson encourages you to reconsider. After all, it's fun to see your name in print! Publishing your writing is the focus of Standards **W.6.6**, **W.7.6**, and **W.8.6**.

The advice that Isaac Asimov offers to writers seeking to publish their work may not seem to be advice you want to take at this point in your writing life, but in fact it is excellent advice, even for a writer with modest ambitions. Asimov, who is most famous as a science fiction novelist, published about 500 books. While you may not have dreams of building a writing career as extensive as Asimov's, publishing your work right now is a very real possibility, and one that you should seriously consider.

For most of Asimov's writing life, publishing meant having his writings appear printed on paper—in newspapers, magazines, and books. And of course we usually think of published works as those appearing on paper. However, the actual definition of *publish* provides a much wider meaning of the term. Take a look at the dictionary definition:

1. to make information available and distribute it to the public

2. to send forth, as a book, newspaper, musical piece, or other printed work, either for sale or for general distribution; to print, and issue from the press

Publishing, then, is making your words and ideas available to others. Remember that you share your words and ideas all the time—in text messages, emails, and social media. Indeed, the ready availability of a variety of social media platforms has created amazing new opportunities for writers (and artists) seeking to make their work visible to others.

Have You Ever Thought of Publishing Your Writing?

The answer is probably *No, never!* (Showing your essays to your parents doesn't exactly count as publishing.) Most students think of writing as something they do only for class assignments. Do you think this way? Do you think that once your essay is written and graded by the teacher, its life is over? Well, think again. You might want to take a bit of Isaac Asimov's advice and try to get something you've written published. Here are some publication ideas to consider.

Local Media

1. Submit your best essay (or write a new one) to a newspaper or news site run by your school or in your local community.

2. Contribute a short story, essay, or poem to a school magazine or to your school's website. If there isn't already a school magazine of student writing, maybe you could start one.

3. Establish a bulletin board in your school hallway where you and other students can post samples of your work.

National Media

There are numerous magazines and websites that publish writing by children and teens; some organizations even sponsor contests with cash prizes. All have websites where you can find the details about how to submit your work. Here's a sampling of some of the best publishers of kids' writing.

1. *Stone Soup* is a magazine made up entirely of the creative work of kids. Young people ages 13 and younger contribute stories, poems, book reviews, and artwork.

2. *New Moon Girls* is created by girls 8 to 14. This advertising-free magazine is committed to showing "how girls are powerful, active, interesting makers in charge of their lives," as its guidelines state. Submissions that don't match an upcoming theme might be published at the magazine's website.

3. *Cricket* offers readers ages 9 to 14 stories, articles, and poems as well as puzzles, crafts, recipes, and activities created by professional writers. Although the magazine does not accept regular submissions by kids, it does run contests to which kids can submit their stories, poetry, essays, and art.

4. *Rattle* is a highly regarded literary magazine that publishes poetry. In 2013, the magazine started soliciting poetry by young people. Work that is accepted is published in a print anthology released in December and is also posted as daily content at the magazine's website.

For a more thorough and up-to-date listing of magazines, websites, anthologies, and contests open to children and teens, see the online resource NewPages Young Authors Guide. NewPages.com is among the top sources of information on literary magazines, independent publishers, writing contests, and other information used by writers at all stages of their careers—from new authors to well-published authors.

. . . .

TIP: Before you send your work to any publication, be sure to read its **writer guidelines**. These tell you what kind of work the publication accepts and how manuscripts should be formatted and submitted. For example, some publications accept work only through email, or only through a specific online platform.

And in most cases, you'll be asked to submit a digital file, which you'll need to create by using a word processor.

Just about every publication makes its writer guidelines available online. Check them out, and follow the instructions. If you don't follow the writer guidelines, you're unlikely to be published.

. . . .

Blogging

For the Internet-savvy and the not-so-Internet-savvy alike, one of the quickest and easiest ways to get your work out into the world is to publish it yourself on a blog! Blogging enables you to connect to an audience, which may consist of just family and friends—or it could be global. Additionally, blogging enables you to engage with this audience through comments and other social media.

Platforms such as WordPress.com are free to use. With these platforms, you can get a domain and template and be published within an hour or less. But before you get started, keep these tips in mind:

- **Never publish personal information about yourself online.**
  Don't publish your full name, address, school, or any other information that someone could use to identify you. Use just your first name or a pseudonym (a false name). Additionally, you might consider creating a password-protected blog and give the password only to those whom you trust.

- **Be kind.** By blogging, you are establishing your public reputation. So think about how you want to be seen by others. It's best to be known as a thoughtful, respectful writer, not a nasty, snarky one.

- **Take caution with photos and videos.** Respect copyright! Publish only photos and videos you took yourself, or photos and videos that are available through a Creative Commons license. Additionally, be sure that you don't publish geolocation data along with your photo, which could be used to identify your location, and check with friends and others before you publish their photos online.

Finally, enjoy yourself! A blog could be a way to share a daily or weekly journal of your life. Or it could be a way to explore and share one of your passions, whether it be for watching movies, skateboarding, or inventing your own cookie recipes. There's sure to be others who have similar interests and will enjoy reading what you have to say on the topic!

Are You Inspired?

Most likely, publishing your writing is a completely new idea for you, but it just might be a real possibility now that you've read this lesson. Remember Isaac Asimov's advice: Keep submitting your work, keep writing, and sooner or later, you are likely to be able to call yourself a published author. Good luck!

Posttest

Now that you've finished the lessons in this book, take this 30-question test. It will give you a sense of what you have learned about writing and the writing process. Give yourself about 30 minutes for the test. Afterward, use the answer key to see how you did. The answer key tells you which lesson addresses the skill or concept that each question represents, so that you know which lessons you might want to return to and reread.

For questions 1–30, circle the letter next to your answer choice.

1. What does knowing the audience for your writing help you decide?
   a. how much to write
   b. what kind of tone to use
   c. how seriously to take the writing project
   d. whether to write by hand or on a computer

2. What is the main purpose of writing an argument?
   a. to show why you are right
   b. to give free rein to your passions
   c. to convince others to agree with your position
   d. to reveal the errors in your opponents' thinking

3. What is the main purpose of writing a narrative?
   a. to make people laugh
   b. to use chronological order
   c. to use dialogue and description
   d. to reveal the importance of an event

4. How does making an idea web differ from brainstorming and free-writing?
   a. With an idea web, you will probably not come up with as many ideas.
   b. With an idea web, you need to think about the relationships between ideas.
   c. With an idea web, you don't need to worry about writing complete sentences.
   d. With an idea web, you need to do other types of prewriting before you can start.

5. You are doing research for an informational text on President Theodore Roosevelt. Which of the following library resources is likely to provide the most in-depth information about his childhood and education?
   a. a biography
   b. an encyclopedia article
   c. the letters he wrote to his own children
   d. the website of his home, now a museum

6. What keywords should be used to check the index of a book on folklore to see what kinds of information it has on Celtic mythology?
   a. folklore
   b. mythology
   c. myths, Celtic
   d. gods, goddesses

7. Which is the BEST thesis statement for an argument on skateboarding written for your local newspaper?
   a. Skateboarding is a growing trend.
   b. Skateboarding is challenging and difficult.
   c. Skateboarding is the most popular sport among my friends.
   d. Skateboarding is a fun sport that deserves respect in our town.

8. Arguments, informational texts, and narratives all include which of the following?
   a. a thesis statement
   b. evidence to support a claim
   c. a beginning, middle, and end
   d. quotations from experts and others

9. It's important that the organizational pattern of an argument includes which of the following?
   a. a discussion of any opposing views
   b. an explanation of the causes and effects of the problem
   c. the sequencing of information in the order of importance
   d. the comparison and contrasting of claims and counterclaims

10. Which of the following is the BEST opening to a narrative about the author's hometown?
    a. Let me tell you about where I was born.
    b. I come from a small town just south of the border with Canada.
    c. Where I come from, the winter nights were long and bejeweled with stars.
    d. The city where I live now may be big and exciting, but I miss my hometown.

11. What quality do well-chosen quotations add to an essay, such as a response to literature?
    a. drama
    b. intimacy
    c. authority
    d. familiarity

12. What special purpose do transitions and words and phrases about time serve in a narrative?
    a. They keep the sequence of events clear.
    b. They engage the reader with sensory details.
    c. They reveal how the problem will be solved.
    d. They help the reader visualize the experience.

13. Which of the following BEST describes an effective conclusion to an essay?

    a. It provides new ideas for the reader to wonder about.

    b. It suggests related topics for one or more future essays.

    c. It asks questions that have been left unanswered in the essay.

    d. It sums up what the reader should have learned from the essay.

Read the following paragraph, and then answer questions 14–18 based on the paragraph.

> What in the heck is a duck-billed platypus? It is true that the scientists who first studied this bizarre creature asked questions like this one, because of their strange bodies. The platypus really does look like a small mammal with the bill of a duck somehow stitched or in some other way stuck on its face. It has other unusual features, such as webbed feet. It is one of only three mammal species that lay eggs. Male platypuses are venomous!

14. Which of the following changes would do the MOST to improve the first sentence of this paragraph?

    a. Change the question to a statement.

    b. Define the term *duck-billed platypus*.

    c. Change "What in the heck" to "What on Earth."

    d. No change

15. Which of the following words or phrases should be deleted from the second sentence of this paragraph?

    a. "It is true that"

    b. "bizarre"

    c. "one"

    d. "because of their strange bodies"

16. Which of the following changes would do the MOST to improve the third sentence of this paragraph?

    a. Delete "small."

    b. Change "the bill of a duck" to "a duck bill."

    c. Change "somehow stitched or in some other way stuck on" to "attached to."

    d. No change

17. Which of the following would be the BEST transition word to add to the beginning of the final sentence of the paragraph?

    a. Yet . . .

    b. For instance . . .

    c. Additionally . . .

    d. In conclusion . . .

18. Which of the following domain-specific terms could be used in making the information in this paragraph more specific?

    a. *cell*, having to do with the most basic structural unit of organisms

    b. *anatomy*, having to do with the structure of the bodies of plants and animals

    c. *skepticism*, having to do with the doubting and questioning attitude of scientists

    d. *ecosystem*, having to do with the interactions of the different organisms in an environment

19. Which of the following sentences is in the passive voice?

    a. The sock was found under the sofa.

    b. The sock was gray with blue stripes.

    c. The sock belonged to my little brother.

    d. The sock was supposed to be put in the hamper.

20. In which of the following sentences is *myself* used as an intensive pronoun, inessential to the overall meaning of sentence?

    a. I myself will write the letter to the principal.

    b. I'll help myself to some of your delicious soup!

    c. I looked at myself in the mirror before going out.

    d. I gave myself a treat for doing so well on the test.

21. Which of the following sentences includes an infinitive used as an adjective?

    a. Violet prefers to walk to school.

    b. My dream is to get the lead in the play.

    c. I cut up some pears to add to our salad.

    d. To get to the playground, go left at the corner.

22. Which of the following is a compound sentence?
   a. James and Eleanor are actually twins.
   b. I wanted ice cream, but he wanted cake.
   c. We could run at the park or swim in the pool.
   d. I want you to tell me the story before you leave!

23. In which of the following sentences are the commas used correctly?
   a. Jessica's only brother, Joseph, is five years old.
   b. What did your brother, Gregory, say to your brother, Norman?
   c. My sister, Emma, likes to sing, and my sister, Amy, plays the piano.
   d. His sister, Stella, goes to my school, while the others go to school with hm.

24. In which of the following sentences is punctuation BEST used to show an unfinished thought?
   a. I can't say what?
   b. I can't say, what.
   c. (I can't say what.)
   d. I can't say what . . .

25. Which of the following practices is recommended to help you proof-read a composition?
   a. Listen to music.
   b. Read the piece out loud.
   c. Use your spell-check program.
   d. Make your best guess when you are unsure.

26. Read this sentence:

   Although students may wear any kind of shoes, they are better off wearing sneakers.

   Which of the following changes should be made to the sentence?
   a. Add a comma after "Although."
   b. Change "may" to "could."
   c. Change "they" to "you."
   d. No change

27. Read this sentence:

Terry's parents did not usually serve desserts after dinner, but it was certainly allowed on her birthday.

Which of the following changes should be made to the sentence?
a. Change "did" to "would."
c. Add a comma after "desserts."
c. Change "it was certainly allowed" to "they certainly did."
d. No change

28. Read this sentence:

I don't care for these boots they are too heavy.

Which of the following changes should be made to the sentence?
a. Add ellipses after "boots."
b. Add a comma after "boots."
c. Add "because" after "boots."
d. No change

29. Read these sentences:

I get so tired in the evenings. Especially on the days when I go to karate class.

Which of the following changes should be made to these sentences?
a. Combine the sentences by changing the period to a comma.
b. Combine the sentences by adding a comma and the conjunction "but."
c. End the first sentence after "tired" and add the phrase "in the evenings" to the second sentence.
d. No change

30. Read this sentence:

Because he was so tired, Miko went to sleep after dinner almost immediately.

Which of the following changes should be made to the sentence?
a. Delete the comma after "tired" and add one after "sleep."
b. Change "went" to "is going to."
c. Move "almost immediately" directly after "sleep."
d. No change

Answer Key

1. **b.** Lesson 1
2. **c.** Lesson 1
3. **d.** Lesson 1
4. **b.** Lesson 4
5. **a.** Lesson 6
6. **c.** Lesson 6
7. **d.** Lesson 7
8. **c.** Lesson 8
9. **a.** Lesson 9
10. **c.** Lesson 11
11. **c.** Lesson 13
12. **a.** Lesson 14
13. **d.** Lesson 15
14. **c.** Lesson 17
15. **a.** Lesson 17
16. **c.** Lesson 17
17. **c.** Lesson 18
18. **c.** Lesson 18
19. **a.** Lesson 20
20. **a.** Lesson 21
21. **c.** Lesson 22
22. **b.** Lesson 23
23. **a.** Lesson 24
24. **d.** Lesson 25
25. **b.** Lesson 26
26. **d.** Lesson 27
27. **c.** Lesson 27
28. **c.** Lesson 27
29. **a.** Lesson 28
30. **c.** Lesson 28

Glossary

This glossary includes definitions for all boldface terms in the book. At the end of each definition, the lesson where the term appears is indicated.

action verb   a word that expresses action, telling what the subject is (or was or will be) doing, such as *smile, want,* or *see* (Lesson 19)

active voice   In the active voice, the subject of the sentence (or clause) is the agent, as in *The girl threw the ball.* Compare with *passive voice.* (Lesson 20)

adjective   a word that modifies a noun, telling *What kind? Which one? How much? How many?* (Lesson 19)

adverb   a word that modifies a verb, an adjective, or another adverb, telling *Where? When? How much? How many?* (Lesson 19)

anecdote   a brief story (Lesson 11)

antecedent   the word or phrase that a pronoun replaces or refers to (Lesson 21)

apostrophe [']   a punctuation mark used in the possessive form of singular and plural nouns (*the girl's sneakers, the girls' locker room*) and to show where letters have been omitted in contractions (*I'm* and *won't*) (Lesson 25)

argument   a piece of writing whose purpose is to persuade readers to take a particular point of view on some subject, or to convince them to take a particular action (Lesson 1)

audience   in writing, the people whom the author expects to read a particular piece of writing (Lesson 1)

body paragraphs   the paragraphs that follow the introduction and lead to the conclusion. They support and develop the central idea. (Lesson 8)

brainstorming   in writing, a process of generating ideas without criticizing or filtering them (Lesson 2)

claim   in an argument, the statement of the writer's point of view or opinion on the topic (Lesson 1)

classify   to group similar things or concepts and assign a name or category to each group (Lesson 9)

clause   a group of words that includes a subject and a verb (Lesson 23)

clichés   phrases that have been used so often that they sound trite and lack energy (Lesson 17)

comma [,]   a punctuation mark used to show a pause or break in a sentence (Lesson 24)

comma splice [*see also:* run-on sentence]   the use of a comma to join two independent clauses in one sentence with no coordinating conjunction (Lesson 24)

common noun   a word that indicates any general person, place, or thing, such as *boy* or *city* (Lesson 19)

compare   to tell about similarities (Lesson 9)

complete sentence   a sentence that includes a subject and predicate and can stand alone (Lesson 28)

complex sentence   a sentence with one main clause and at least one subordinate clause (Lesson 23)

composition   a piece of writing (Lesson 1)

compound sentence   a sentence with two or more main clauses (Lesson 23)

compound-complex sentence   a sentence with two or more main clauses and at least one subordinate clause (Lesson 23)

conclusion   the ending of a composition, often a paragraph long. It sums up or otherwise ends the composition. (Lesson 8)

conditional mood   Verbs in the conditional mood tell about situations that are dependent on hypothetical or otherwise unreal conditions; for example: *If I had tickets to the show, I would go.* The modal verbs *would, could,* or *might* are used to express the conditional mood. (Lesson 20)

contrast to tell about differences (Lesson 9)

coordinate adjectives adjectives that each modify the same noun equally (e.g., *bright, shining star*); their order can be reversed, and they can be joined with the word *and* (Lesson 24)

coordinating conjunction The coordinating conjunctions are *and, but, for, nor, or, so,* and *yet.* They are used to join similar elements in a sentence, such as two independent clauses. (Lesson 23)

dash [—] a punctuation mark used to emphasize a pause or break in thought or speech (Lesson 25)

dangling modifier a modifier whose subject is not named anywhere in the sentence; for example: *Tumbling down the stairs, his heavy coat kept him from getting hurt.* (Lesson 28)

definition a piece of writing (brief or lengthy) that tells about the meaning or significance of a word, phrase, or concept (Lesson 9)

dependent clause [*also:* subordinate clause] a clause that does not express a complete thought and cannot stand alone; for example: *While Ellen slept.* Compare with *independent clause.* (Lesson 23)

domain-specific vocabulary words that are specific to a particular subject area (Lesson 18)

draft *n.* a provisional, or temporary, version of a composition; *v.* to write a provisional, or temporary, version of a composition (Lesson 11)

drama a composition, or piece of writing, written for performance, usually by actors in a theater (Lesson 1)

edit to look closely at a piece of writing in order to revise and correct it; in this book, we use the word *editing* to refer specifically to the stage in the writing process when the writer revises for effective language use (Lesson 16)

ellipses [. . .] a punctuation mark used to show a pause or break in thought or speech or to show that words have been left out of a quotation (Lesson 25)

essay originally, a form of reflective writing developed by the 16th-century French writer Michel de Montaigne; now, a composition that states a main idea, supports that idea, and builds to a conclusion (Lesson 1)

evidence in an argument, the information, examples, and quotations given to support the claim (Lesson 13)

expository text a piece of writing whose purpose is to explain (Lesson 1)

fragment an incomplete sentence (Lesson 28)

freewriting   the practice of writing continuously, usually in a timed session, without stopping to correct your spelling, language use, or sentence structure (Lesson 3)

gerund   a verbal that ends with *–ing* and functions as a noun (Lesson 22)

idea web   a visual form or method of prewriting that shows the relationships between different ideas (Lesson 4)

imperative mood   Verbs in the imperative mood give commands; for example: *Remember to get tickets for the show*. The subject (*you*) is typically not named in the sentence but is understood. (Lesson 20)

independent clause [*also:* main clause]   a clause that expresses a complete thought and can stand alone; for example: *Ellen slept*. Compare with *dependent clause*. (Lesson 23)

indicative mood   Verbs in the indicative mood tell about what is real or observed to be true; for example: *I wanted to go to the show, but the tickets were sold out*. Most verbs that we use are in the indicative mood. (Lesson 20)

indirect quotation   the restating of something that someone else has said without using their exact words; quotation marks are not used (Lesson 25)

infinitive   a verbal that typically includes the word *to* followed by the simplest form of a verb (e.g., *to see* or *to walk*) and that functions as a noun, adjective, or adverb (Lesson 22)

informational text   a piece of writing whose purpose is to inform (Lesson 1)

intensive pronoun   a pronoun that has the same form as a reflexive pronoun and that is used for emphasis; for example: *I myself will be going there tomorrow*. (Lesson 21)

interrogative mood   Verbs in the interrogative mood pose questions; for examplee: *Do you have tickets for the show?* (Lesson 20)

interrogative pronoun   The interrogative pronouns are *who* (nominative), *whom* (objective), *whose* (possessive), *which*, and *what*. They are used in questions. (Lesson 21)

introduction   the beginning of a composition, often a paragraph long. It sets the scene or introduces the topic and central idea. (Lesson 8)

journaling   a personal and often private form of writing, in which the author tells about and reflects on his or her observations and experiences (Lesson 1)

keywords   terms that identify important ideas related to a research topic or question (Lesson 6)

letter   a composition, or piece of writing, written to communicate directly with a person or organization, typically delivered through the mail (Lesson 1)

linking verbs   a verb that tells what the subject is (or was or will be); the most common linking verb is *be* (Lesson 19)

misplaced modifier   a modifier (adjective, adverb, or modifying phrase or clause) that does not appear near the word it modifies (Lesson 28)

mood   The mood of a verb can show certainty, uncertainty, wishes, commands, or other attitudes. The common moods in the English language are the indicative, imperative, interrogative, conditional, and subjunctive. (Lesson 20)

narrative   a piece of writing that tells about real or imagined experiences and whose purpose is to tell a story or explore the significance of an event (Lesson 1)

narrative technique   a method used to tell a story, such as description and dialogue (Lesson 14)

nonrestrictive elements   words, phrases, or clauses that give information that is not necessary for the overall meaning of a sentence (Lesson 24)

noun   a word that names persons, places, things, and states or qualities (Lesson 19)

objective case   Pronouns in the objective case are used as objects of verbs and prepositions; for example: *me, you, him, her, it, us,* and *them.* (Lesson 21)

on-demand writing task [*also:* response to a prompt]   a writing assignment that requires you to write in response to a prompt and within a limited timeframe, usually a single sitting (Lesson 10)

organizational pattern   a method of organizing or sequencing information that helps to guide readers through a piece of writing (Lesson 9)

parentheses [( )]   punctuation marks used to set off dates and citations as well as other nonessential information (Lesson 25)

participle   a verbal that ends with *–ing*, ends with *–ed*, or takes an irregular form (such as *brought, done,* and *known*) and that functions as an adjective (Lesson 22)

passive voice   In the passive voice, the subject is the recipient of the action expressed by the verb, as in *The ball was thrown by the girl*. Compare with *active voice*. (Lesson 20)

personal narrative   a narrative that tells about an actual experience rather than an imagined one (Lesson 7)

phrase   a small group of words, often acting as a unit within a sentence (Lesson 23)

poetry   a composition, or piece of writing, that reflects the author's special care with language, often written in the lyric mode, aimed at expressing the experience and feelings of a first-person speaker (Lesson 1)

possessive case   Pronouns in the possessive case are used to replace possessive nouns; for example, *The toothbrush is my sister's* becomes *The toothbrush is hers*. (Lesson 21)

predicate   the part of a sentence that includes the verb and its modifiers (Lesson 28)

prefix   a word part added to the beginning of a word (Lesson 26)

prepositional phrase   a phrase that includes a preposition and its object (Lesson 23)

prewriting   the activities done at the beginning of a writing project, before drafting. These activities include brainstorming, freewriting, creating idea webs, and outlining. (Section 1 introduction)

prompt   in writing, a question or assignment intended to elicit a particular kind of response (Lesson 1)

pronoun   a word that takes the place of a noun or noun phrase in a sentence (Lesson 21)

proofread   to take one last, close look at a composition in order to find and correct any misspellings, mistakes in punctuation, and other small errors (Lesson 16)

proper noun   a word that names a specific person, place, or thing and is capitalized, such as *Fred* or *New York City* (Lesson 19)

purpose   in writing, the author's reason for writing (Lesson 1)

quotation marks ["”]   punctuation marks that are used to show the use or citation of exact words from another person or text (Lesson 25)

reflexive pronoun   a pronoun that shows that the subject of a verb is also receiving the action; for example *Jeanine made the drawing for herself*. (Lesson 21)

relative pronoun   The relative pronouns include *who, whom, whose, which,* and *that,* as well as *whoever, whomever,* and *whichever.* They are used to join dependent and independent clauses or join a clause with its antecedent. (Lesson 21)

research   the process of investigating a subject or question (Lesson 6)

research paper   a form that may present an argument or analysis of a subject based on the investigation of primary and secondary sources (Lesson 1)

response to literature   a specific kind of argument in which the author shares his or her understanding of one or more works of literature (Lesson 1)

response to a prompt [*also:* on-demand writing task]   a composition written to fulfill the requirements of a prompt, usually in a single sitting (Lesson 1)

revise   to make substantial improvements to a piece of writing (Lesson 16)

rough draft   the first, least finished version of a composition (Lesson 11)

run-on sentence [*see also:* comma splice]   a sentence in which two independent clauses are joined without a comma or coordinating adjective (Lesson 28)

sentence fragment   an incomplete sentence (Lesson 28)

simple sentence   a sentence with one main clause (Lesson 23)

slang   informal language (Lesson 17)

subject   the noun or noun phrase that a sentence tells about (Lesson 28)

subjective case   Pronouns in the subjective case are used as subjects of verbs; for example: *I, you, he, she, it, we,* and *they.* (Lesson 21)

subjunctive mood   Verbs in the subjunctive mood are used to express conditions that are not true, in clauses beginning with *if,* after verbs that express a wish, and in subordinate clauses that express an order or recommendation; for example: *If I were you, I would buy tickets as soon as possible.* (Lesson 20)

suffix   a word part added to the ending of a word (Lesson 26)

thesis statement   a statement that presents the central idea or claim that the writer intends to support in an essay (Lesson 5)

tone   the quality of the author's (or narrator's) voice, which shows the attitude of the author or narrator toward the subject (Lesson 1)

transition   a word, phrase, or sentence that shows the relationship between ideas or events in a text (Lesson 13)

trigger   something that stimulates writing (Lesson 2)

verb   a word that expresses an action or state of being (Lesson 19)

verbal   a form of a verb that does not function as a verb within a sentence (Lesson 22)

working thesis statement   a general and temporary statement of the central idea of a piece of writing, written during the prewriting process (Lesson 5)

writing process   the series of activities that begins with prewriting and concludes with a finished composition and includes planning, drafting, revising, editing, and proofreading (Lesson 2)

Additional Online Practice

Using the codes below, you'll be able to log in and access additional online practice materials!

Your free online practice access codes are:
FVETE4U72G6E73CRJJ0W
FVE32D843UTC7OT02FNS
FVEG3TIQGC11OVBDO46F
FVEF5E5SHY15C025S2IM

Follow these simple steps to redeem your codes:

- Go to **www.learningexpresshub.com/affiliate** and have your access codes handy.

If you're a new user:
- Click the **New user? Register here** button and complete the registration form to create your account and access your products.
- Be sure to enter your unique access code only once. If you have multiple access codes, you can enter them all—just use a comma to separate each code.
- The next time you visit, simply click the **Returning user? Sign in** button and enter your username and password.
- Do not re-enter previously redeemed access codes. Any products you previously accessed are saved in the **My Account** section on the site. Entering a previously redeemed access code will result in an error message.

If you're a returning user:
- Click the **Returning user? Sign in** button, enter your username and password, and click **Sign In**.
- You will automatically be brought to the **My Account** page to access your products.
- Do not re-enter previously redeemed access codes. Any products you previously accessed are saved in the **My Account** section on the site. Entering a previously redeemed access code will result in an error message.

If you're a returning user with a new access code:
- Click the **Returning user? Sign in** button, enter your username, password, and new access code, and click **Sign In**.
- If you have multiple access codes, you can enter them all—just use a comma to separate each code.
- Do not re-enter previously redeemed access codes. Any products you previously accessed are saved in the **My Account** section on the site. Entering a previously redeemed access code will result in an error message.

If you have any questions, please contact Customer Support at Support@ebsco.com. All inquiries will be responded to within a 24-hour period during our normal business hours: 9:00 A.M.–5:00 P.M. Eastern Time. Thank you!

Notes